A STUDY OF THE BOOK OF L

MW00737223

CAN I BE
honest?

HOW TO PROCESS AND EXPRESS YOUR EMOTIONS IN A BIBLICAL WAY

Written by Kayla Ferris

> # WE MUST EXCHANGE WHISPERS WITH GOD BEFORE SHOUTS WITH THE WORLD.
>
> *Lysa TerKeurst*

Pair your study guide with the First 5 mobile app!

This study guide is designed to accompany your study of Scripture in the First 5 mobile app. You can use it as a standalone study or as an accompanying guide to the daily content within First 5.

First 5 is a free mobile app developed by Proverbs 31 Ministries to transform your daily time with God.

Go to the app store on your smartphone, download the First 5 app, and create a free account!

www.first5.org

let us lift up our
hearts & our hands
to God in heaven...

Lamentations 3:41

WELCOME *to* LAMENTATIONS

I was sitting in the family room with my four daughters, the television playing in the background, when the local news came on. I halfway paid attention as stories about this shooting, that fatal car accident, criminal mug shots and candlelight vigils rolled across the screen.

One of my daughters finally said, "Hey, Mom, can we turn this off? It's scary and sad."

Scared and sad are not my favorite feelings — along with worried, lonely, confused or angry. Yet I will experience every single one of these emotions in my lifetime. Sometimes I might even feel them all at the same time. Maybe I will even feel them toward God.

That might seem like an inappropriate thing to say. Most of us do not want to admit feeling these negative emotions at all, especially not toward God. What might people think of us if we were really honest about our emotions? Or even more importantly, how might God react?!

Sometimes we need permission to feel our feelings. This is healthy. But when that takes place and we are ready to process and express those emotions, how do we do so in a biblical, God-honoring way? Thankfully, God gives us a guide in the book of Lamentations.

The words of Lamentations are beautifully poetic, but they are also raw and painful. Jerusalem faced a devastating enemy. On the surface, we might think the enemy was Babylon or even God, but the real enemy was their sin. Sin always leaves behind a mess of death and pain. Within Lamentations, we will see the immense fear, sadness and anger that come from living in a broken, sin-filled world. There will be glimpses of hope ... but they remain only that: glimpses. That is, until we flip out of Lamentations into later books in our Bibles — books that mention a virgin giving birth to a son named Jesus — and we realize He is the only real hope this world has. We catch one such glimpse of hope in Christ in Lamentations 3:25: *"The LORD is good to those who wait for him, to the soul who seeks him."*

Maybe you need hope today. Maybe you are looking for a way to process what you are feeling while still keeping your eyes on Jesus. Or maybe you aren't doing this study for your own pain but because you want to walk well with the people in your life who are hurting and heavy-hearted. Whatever it is you are feeling, God cares. God created emotions! How much more than us must He understand them? In Hosea 11:8-9 we see a range of emotions as God said about Himself, *"My heart recoils within me; my compassion grows warm and tender. I will not execute my burning anger ..."* God wants us to know that He understands what it's like to feel. And He is ready for you to bring everything inside of you and set it before Him. He will teach you how to process any emotion you carry today with honesty and grace. He will love you in your pain. And He will walk you through.

Welcome to the book of Lamentations.

— Kayla

WHO WROTE LAMENTATIONS?

Lamentations is a poetic and artistic look into the deep sorrows and pain felt by the Jewish people in 586 B.C. when they were overthrown by Babylon. Who was the poet who masterfully constructed these lines of emotion? In truth, we do not know. The Hebrew Scriptures do not name an author for this book. For that reason, we can only definitively say that this book is anonymous.

However, there are many scholars who believe Jeremiah to be the author. This dates back to ancient Jewish tradition. The Greek translation of the Hebrew Scriptures (called the Septuagint, which was written around 2 B.C.) attributes the writing of Lamentations to Jeremiah. You can still see this reflected in the King James Version of the Bible, as it titles this book "The Lamentations of Jeremiah." There are certainly many similarities between the writings of Lamentations and Jeremiah. Second Chronicles 35:25 also specifically talks about Jeremiah composing a lament (although this was not necessarily the book of Lamentations), so we know he was certainly capable of writing this book. This long-held assumption about Jeremiah as the author is also why we find the book of Lamentations immediately following Jeremiah's book in our Bibles.

Yet in the past 200 years or so, scholars have questioned this long-held belief about the authorship of Lamentations. There are differences in key vocabulary between the book of Jeremiah and the book of Lamentations as well as details from Jeremiah's life that do not seem to correlate with Lamentations' style and timing. For example, Lamentations 4:20 speaks of King Zedekiah's capture by saying *"the breath of our nostrils, the LORD's anointed, was captured in their pits,"* and some scholars argue that Jeremiah, a vocal critic of the king, would not have spoken of Zedekiah in such positive words. Also, this verse appears to be an eyewitness account, but Jeremiah was imprisoned during this time. Therefore, perhaps the best way to study Lamentations is to see the author as an anonymous poet commissioned by God to record, process and express the hard and deep emotions of Jerusalem. It is because of this writer, whoever he was, that we are allowed to peek behind the curtain into the very real and raw pain of God's people, and we can walk away knowing that we can come before God honestly as well.

Perhaps the best way to study Lamentations is to see the author as an anonymous poet commissioned by God to record, process and express the hard and deep emotions of Jerusalem.

LIFE IN ISRAEL at the TIME of LAMENTATIONS

In order to understand the scope and cause for lament in this book, it is important to know the history of Israel, both leading up to and surrounding the events of Lamentations.

When God called Israel (first through their patriarch Abraham and his family, and then through Moses and other leaders) to become His set-apart nation, He gave them covenants (Genesis 12:1-3; Exodus 19:3-6). The people had a special role to play in showing God to the entire world. As such, God would guide and protect them **so long as** the people stayed loyal to God and His ways. If they did not, God warned them of the serious consequences.

After God brought His people out of slavery in Egypt, they immediately started off on the wrong foot, creating and worshipping an idol at the bottom of Mount Sinai in Exodus 32. Then they rebelled in the wilderness (e.g., Numbers 14), they failed to obey God while taking the promised land of Canaan (e.g., Joshua 7), and they went astray over and over in the time of the judges. God continued to send warnings and call them back.

Some people thought an earthly king would help them, so God allowed kings (1 Samuel 8). At first it seemed to work. However, the kingdom of Israel eventually split in two, and the often sinful kings showed the spiraling of God's people away from Him. No matter how many prophets or warnings God sent, the people refused to come back. And the consequences of their actions soon followed.

The southern kingdom of Judah held the city of Jerusalem and therefore the temple of God. Jerusalem had survived numerous attacks through the years, including attacks from Assyria. However, in the sixth century B.C., a new power was on the rise: Babylon, with its young king, Nebuchadnezzar, was

looking to expand its kingdom and might. In 605 B.C., Nebuchadnezzar defeated Egypt, and Jeremiah tried to give warning to the nation of Judah, to no avail. A portion of citizens were taken off to Babylon.

The final king of Israel, Zedekiah, eventually decided to lead his own rebellion against Babylon, to disastrous effect. Nebuchadnezzar had enough and decided to finish Judah once and for all. Babylon invaded and destroyed what archaeologists suggest were around 80% of all the towns and villages in Judah during this time period.[1] That is an astonishing amount! They then held an 18-month siege against Jerusalem. This caused starvation, death and disease to become rampant. Finally, in 586 B.C., the Babylonians broke through the walls of Jerusalem and destroyed and/or burned the palaces, homes, walls and temple of God's people (2 Kings 24-25). Those who had miraculously survived both the starvation and the slaughter were marched to Babylon on foot, walking a thousand-mile journey into a foreign land.

The book of Lamentations is an eyewitness account of the atrocities Jerusalem faced at this moment in history.

Editor's Note: This study discusses war in ancient Israel but does not reflect opinions, conclusions or commentary about present-day events. We stand with all those suffering today and grieve the losses of image bearers of God across the world. By studying His Word together, we pray God will lead us in how to process and respond to all circumstances with the love of Christ.

OLD TESTAMENT BIBLE TIMELINE

God's Covenant
With Abraham

ca. 2100 B.C.

The Divided
Kingdom: North
(Israel) & South
(Judah)

ca. 930 B.C.

The Judges

ca. 1399 B.C.

The Kings: Saul,
David & Solomon

ca. 1050 B.C.

Creation

Israel's Exodus
From Egypt,
Ten Commandments,
Settling Into Canaan

ca. 1450 B.C.

Lamentations is written

The Fall of Judah to Babylon
ca. 586 B.C.

Return From Exile To Rebuild the Temple and Wall in Jerusalem
ca. 539-430 B.C.

Exile
ca. 586-539 B.C.

The Fall of Israel to Assyria
ca. 722 B.C.

End of the Old Testament

Lament Defined

Lament (verb):
to mourn and cry with groans of sadness, to express grief verbally.[1]

Lament (noun):
a formal expression of sorrow or mourning, especially in verse or song; an elegy or dirge.[2]

Each chapter of the book of Lamentations is considered a lament. There are also several examples of lament found in the book of Psalms. See Psalm 44 or Psalm 74 for two examples.

POETIC STRUCTURE
of LAMENTATIONS

Lamentations is unique in that it is an entire book dedicated to lament, whereas other books of the Bible (for instance, Psalms) may include some lament but are not totally dedicated to mourning. Within the formal expression of mourning in Lamentations, we find a complex and beautiful poetic structure, which we can see even more richly when we look at our English translation alongside the original Hebrew. Knowing this structure can give us a deeper appreciation for the artistry within this book.

Acrostic

An acrostic poem is a poem in which the first word of each line starts with a successive letter of the alphabet. In English, this would mean the first line would start with the letter A, the second line with the letter B, and so on. Lamentations was written as an acrostic poem in Hebrew, starting with the letter *alef* and ending with the letter *tav*. (See the "Hebrew Alphabet Guide" on page 14 for reference.)

Because there are 22 letters in the Hebrew alphabet, Chapters 1, 2 and 4 of Lamentations all contain 22 verses, one verse per letter. Chapter 5 also contains 22 verses although it breaks from the acrostic nature. Chapter 3 contains 66 verses while still following the acrostic form; instead of one verse per letter, the poet wrote three verses per letter. So each line in Lamentations 3:1-3 begins with *alef* while each line in Lamentations 3:4-6 begins with *beit*, and so on. To write and flow in acrostic form takes great skill.

Chiasm

Chiasm is a literary structure where parallel elements correspond in an inverted order. Think of it as a pattern like this: A B C B A. In a chiastic structure, *the point at the center is the central idea*. It is like the mountain peak of the piece. (In the example pattern, this would be the C.)

In Lamentations, the center of the book is Chapter 3. You can see the emphasis on Chapter 3 also by the increased intensity of the acrostic. Chapter 3 is meant to be seen as the highlight of this poetic book. We will find that Chapter 3 is the chapter that contains the most hope.

Qinah *Meter*

In poetry, "meter" refers to the rhythm of the words or syllables. In ancient times, a particular meter called *qinah* was often used in Hebrew poems or psalms that mourned the dead. *Qinah* is a rhythm of two unequal parts. The first part usually contains three syllables. The second part usually contains two syllables. Therefore, the beat sounded something like this: 1-2-3 | 1-2 | 1-2-3 | 1-2. This was meant to create a limping effect, almost "as if the reader is walking haltingly along behind a funeral procession."[1]

Characters

Within Lamentations, the writer also added to the poetic structure by creating several different voices or characters to speak through.

*   **The poet**, who we might think of as the primary speaker in Lamentations, tells the events. The poet will speak both about and to Jerusalem.

*   **Jerusalem** is personified as a woman throughout Lamentations and is often referred to as "*daughter of Zion*." Occasionally, Jerusalem herself will speak up in the book.

*   **"The man who has seen affliction"** (Lamentations 3:1) is an eyewitness character in Chapter 3 who speaks up to tell about what he personally witnessed and the conclusions he came to.

HEBREW ALPHABET
Guide

ט	ח	ז	ו	ה	ד	ג	ב	א
Teit	*Cheit*	*Zayin*	*Vav*	*Hei*	*Dalet*	*Gimel*	*Beit*	*Alef*
(T)	(Ch)	(Z)	(V/O/U)	(H)	(D)	(G)	(B/V)	(Silent)

ס	ן	נ	ם	מ	ל	ך	כ	י
Samekh	*Nun*	*Nun*	*Mem*	*Mem*	*Lamed*	*Khaf*	*Kaf*	*Yod*
(S)	(N)	(N)	(M)	(M)	(L)	(Kh)	(K/Kh)	(Y)

ת	ש	ר	ק	ץ	צ	ף	פ	ע
Tav	*Shin*	*Reish*	*Qof*	*Tzadei*	*Tzadei*	*Fei*	*Pei*	*Ayin*
(T/S)	(Sh/S)	(R)	(Q)	(Tz)	(Tz)	(F)	(P/F)	(Silent)

Ancient Hebrew is read from the right to the left. As you can see from this diagram, the first letter of the Hebrew alphabet is the letter *alef*. The second letter is *beit*. This is where we get our term "**alphabet**"!

If you're counting letters, you'll remember we said there are 22, so why are there 27 in this chart? That is because five sets of these are the same letter. Notice the repeated names: 1) *kaf/khaf*, 2) *mem*, 3) *nun*, 4) *pei/fei* and 5) *tzadei*. Reading from right to left, this chart shows different forms of these letters when used within a word and at the end of a word, respectively.

WHAT YOU HAVE TO LOOK FORWARD TO
in This Guide

Daily Teachings and Questions

Each week of this study includes daily teachings on five passages from Lamentations. Together, we'll walk through the whole book, asking God to teach us through His Word and help us process our emotions today. On each day, you'll also find a set of questions to help guide you through your personal study.

Study Like a Poet

Because Lamentations is written as an acrostic poem, we, too, are going to build our own acrostic to the Lord. At the end of each study day, you will be asked to write one sentence to the Lord that begins with a certain letter of the alphabet. By the end of this study, you will have a sentence for all 26 letters of the English language.

Biblical Highlights

Also within each day, you will find occasional "Biblical Highlight" boxes. These boxes contain brief facts, bonus materials or reflections to ponder as you go along.

Weekend Reflection and Prayer

We are going to use our weekends to spend time in prayer guided by what we have studied in Lamentations. At the end of each week, you will find a guided prayer, inspired by three verses from that week, which you can use for reflection or to focus your prayer time.

Biblically Expressing Emotions

At the end of our study, we've also included a bonus resource with additional insights from Lamentations and other Bible passages that teach us about God's design for processing our emotions in a healthy way.

MAJOR MOMENTS

Week 1

LAMENTATIONS 1:1–2   The once-great city of Jerusalem was no more.

LAMENTATIONS 1:3–7   Jerusalem was afflicted because of her transgressions.

LAMENTATIONS 1:8–11   Jerusalem became naked before her enemies.

LAMENTATIONS 1:12–17   Jerusalem had no one to comfort her.

LAMENTATIONS 1:18–19   Jerusalem acknowledged that God was right in His judgment.

Week 2

LAMENTATIONS 1:20–22   Jerusalem wanted vengeance for her pain.

LAMENTATIONS 2:1–5   God became like an enemy.

LAMENTATIONS 2:6–10   Without the temple, the people felt far from God.

LAMENTATIONS 2:11–14   Children suffering was a cause for lament.

LAMENTATIONS 2:15–19   Though God had allowed the destruction, God was also the only One who could save.

Week 3

LAMENTATIONS 2:20–22   Jerusalem questioned God.

LAMENTATIONS 3:1–9   A firsthand witness felt trapped by God.

LAMENTATIONS 3:10–20   The speaker said his hope had perished.

LAMENTATIONS 3:21–24   The speaker called to mind the steadfast love of the Lord.

LAMENTATIONS 3:25–30   The speaker said it is good to wait on God's salvation.

Week 4

LAMENTATIONS 3:31–33	God is full of compassion and love.
LAMENTATIONS 3:34–39	God seeks justice and is sovereign.
LAMENTATIONS 3:40–42	The speaker encouraged others to return to the Lord.
LAMENTATIONS 3:43–48	The speaker turned his pain toward God.
LAMENTATIONS 3:49–58	God heard the pleas and said, *"Do not fear!"*

Week 5

LAMENTATIONS 3:59–66	The speaker knew God had seen the wrong done to him.
LAMENTATIONS 4:1–10	The gold that was God's people had grown dim.
LAMENTATIONS 4:11–22	God's wrath was complete.
LAMENTATIONS 5:1–14	The people prayed for God to remember.
LAMENTATIONS 5:15–22	The people prayed for God to restore.

WEEK

One

DAY 1

The once-great city of Jerusalem was no more.
LAMENTATIONS 1:1–2

Lamentations wastes no time in expressing emotion. The book opens by describing Jerusalem's destruction and pain. You might notice that Jerusalem is personified as a woman throughout this section, which further intensifies and humanizes the emotion.

• The first two verses of Lamentations 1 are full of contrasts. Let's pull out each one.

Verse 1 says the city used to be "*full of*" what? **people**	But now how did it "*sit*"? **lonely**
Verse 1 says the city used to be what "*among the nations*"? **Great**	But now what was the city "*like*"? ~~Bittttt~~ **a widow**
Verse 1 also says the city was what "*among the provinces*"? **princess**	But now what had she become? **a slave**
The end of verse 2 says who "*dealt treacherously with her*"? **friends**	What had her friends become? **became her enemies**

Jerusalem was once a great and mighty city with influence and growth. Then came devastation that changed everything. This is a reminder that no one is exempt from loss or pain. No amount of money or power or influence can stop loss from touching us. Suffering is one of the things we all collectively share in being human — we all experience pain at some time, in some way.

Lamentations also demonstrates that mourning is complex and layered. And sometimes what we mourn is not only a tangible thing or person we have lost but also the loss of the way life used to be. Taking a cue from Lamentations today, let's break down and identify some losses we feel.

- Think of a loss you have experienced in your life or that someone close to you might be experiencing.

What was life like before the loss?	What is missing now? And how do you feel about that?
excitement, expectancy, vision focussed for the future	*excitement has turned to stress & worry.* *I feel sad & that I want to be more positive. & view it as a blessing from God.*

Verse 2 of today's reading says, "*She weeps bitterly in the night … among all her lovers she has none to comfort her.*" Nights can be hard when we are hurting and alone. But they're much harder when we're searching for comfort and companionship in all the wrong places.

- Keeping in mind that the "*she*" in Lamentations 1 refers to Jerusalem, or God's people, what do we learn from Judges 2:17 and 1 Chronicles 5:25 about the kinds of "*lovers*" they turned to for comfort?

They turned to idols & turned away from God.
They were unfaithful to God

Idolatry is not a minor issue in the eyes of God. It's a heartbreaking, destructive mistake He doesn't want to see His children make, which is why it's the first (and second) thing He forbids in the Ten Commandments (Exodus 20:3-4). All of our idols — anything we worship and serve other than God — will fail us in our pain. They will not comfort us.

- Thankfully, in John 16:22, Jesus says, "*So also you have sorrow now, but I will see you again, and your hearts will rejoice, and no one will take your joy from you.*" What two contrasting emotions do we find here, and what do we have to look forward to if we turn to Jesus for love and comfort?

> Sorrow <u>verses</u> rejoicing
>
> we have to look forward to rejoicing when we see him again a when we seek him, no one can take our joy.

A

As we journey through Lamentations, let's build our own acrostic day by day. Write a sentence to the Lord, either your own lament or another kind of prayer based on today's scriptures, starting with the letter A.

> Awaken my soul to sing your praises. May they come off my lips as shouts

DAY 2

As we begin today, let's take a moment to have an honest look at some of our own emotions.

- Have you ever found yourself angry at God? What words did you use to talk to Him about your anger — or if you didn't talk to Him, why not?

yes of course. "How could you God"
" How could you say you
love me & do this"

Even as Christians, we often feel guilt or shame because of our feelings about suffering. Many times we don't share them with others or even with God because we don't want our faith to seem shaky.

- Yet read the words of Psalm 10:1, Psalm 74:1 and Matthew 27:46. What common questions do each of these ask of God?

Why have you LEFT me?
Why do I feel alone?

In today's reading, the writer of Lamentations is going to bring some hard accusations to God. In this particular case, there was a hard truth as to why destruction and pain were happening to the people of Jerusalem.

- Lamentations 1:5 says destruction had come down on them because who had afflicted Jerusalem? For what reason?

The Lord afflicted Jerusalem
because of her multitude of
transgressions

In looking at this verse, we see God did afflict His people — but we are also reminded of a gentle truth about the causes and purposes of that affliction. After God had promised blessings for obedience and curses for disobedience in the past, in Exodus 24:3, *"Moses came and told the people all the words of the LORD and all the rules. And all the people answered with one voice and said, 'All the words that the LORD has spoken we will do.'"* And again in Exodus 24:7, *"they said, 'All that the LORD has spoken we will do, and we will be obedient.'"* But the people didn't do what they promised. Only God kept His word: He said there would be serious consequences of discipline if they sinned, and He was faithful to His promise. Here in Lamentations 1, Jerusalem was afflicted *"for the multitude of her transgressions"* (v. 5).

- What does Hebrews 12:9-13 tell us about how and why God disciplines us? According to Psalm 23:2-3, where does He want to lead us?

> God disciplines us for our betterment.
> He does what is best for us even when its hard in the moment -
>
> - He wants to lead us to the path of righteousness.

In sections of scripture like today's, it is helpful to remember that our God is sovereign. "Sovereignty" means having all power and authority. Reflect on Job 38 when you need to be reminded of the sovereignty of God.

It's also important to understand that there are many reasons for suffering in the world — and *not all suffering we experience is a punishment from God for sins we have committed.* We are not always given the answers to why a sovereign God allows painful things to happen. And that can be so very hard. This hurting, broken world causes us such pain because sin, which leads to death, has infected life here.

But, friend, if God kept His word to justly deliver the consequences of sin like Lamentations says, He will also keep His word to forgive, strengthen and comfort His people.

• Today, God has made these promises:

Romans 6:23:	eternal life
1 Peter 2:24:	healing
Revelation 21:4:	No more death, sorrow, pain & suffering
1 Corinthians 15:54-55:	victory !
Psalm 56:8-9:	God is for me !

We might not always have an answer to why bad things happen, but we can trust God when He says He is "*near to the brokenhearted*" (Psalm 34:18).

B

As we journey through Lamentations, let's build our own acrostic day by day. Write a sentence to the Lord, either your own lament or another kind of prayer based on today's scriptures, starting with the letter B.

Break down the walls of my heart so that I will want to be more like you.

DAY 3

In Lamentations 1:8, we are reminded again that Jerusalem's suffering stemmed from her sins. We have touched on the fact that not all of our suffering is a direct result of some specific sin in our lives; however, sin in the world has caused suffering. And Jerusalem's sin of turning away from the Lord is described here in vivid language.

BIBLICAL HIGHLIGHT:

Lamentations 1:9 says, "She took no thought of her future ..." *Oh, the sorrows we could save ourselves from if we could keep our minds focused not just on what we want now but on what our actions mean for the future, both on earth and in eternity (1 Timothy 6:18-19)!*

- According to verse 8, "*she became filthy.*" Those who honored her then "*despise[d] her.*" What did they see? And what was her reaction?

  They have seen her nakedness.
  c she sighs & turns away

To understand this as fully as possible, we may need a little cultural context. According to biblical scholar Christopher Wright, in surrounding cultures during this time, women caught in adultery were sometimes shamed by having their skirts pulled up in public.[1] To be clear, this is *not* a practice Scripture condones — but if we think of how this would feel, it's hard to imagine such humiliation.

- We have all had times when we have experienced shame. What does shame feel like to you?

  - Shame is embarassing
  - like I want to crawl in a
  hole & never come out.

- Read John 19:23. What did the soldiers take from Jesus as He was being crucified? How would this have left Him?

They took his garmets.　　*it left him naked*

This image of Jesus is similar to the verses we read in Lamentations today. The difference is that *"Jerusalem sinned grievously; **therefore** she became filthy"* (v. 8, emphasis added). Jesus never sinned and yet suffered anyway on behalf of you and me.

Notice in Lamentations 1:9 and verse 11, there are quotation marks around the lines at the end. These were direct cries from Jerusalem to the Lord to express what the people were feeling.

- What are some of the feelings expressed in the quotations of verses 9 and 11?

the enemy triumphed. , sad.　　　?

- Read Isaiah 53:3-4. These verses are a prophecy of the suffering servant, who is Jesus. These words then describe what Jesus felt during His time on earth. What emotions are present in these verses?

rejection , grief, sorrow , sadness

Like the people we read about in Lamentations, in this life, we sometimes feel shame, rejection, humiliation or loneliness. What is so amazing is that Jesus chose to identify Himself with us in these emotions. Hebrews 4:15 says, *"For we do not have a high priest who is unable to sympathize with our weaknesses, but one who in every respect has been tempted as we are, yet without sin."* When we need an example of the best ways to process and express emotions, we need only look to Jesus.

- Back to Isaiah 53. According to verses 8 and 12, why did Jesus go through all of this humiliation and pain?

He did it for us. He took our sin on the cross.

Romans 9:33 says "*whoever believes in him will not be put to shame.*" Jesus took our shame and carried it on the cross so you and I would never have to carry it again. Now we can bring all of our emotions and lay them down before Jesus, who understands. What a gift!

C

As we journey through Lamentations, let's build our own acrostic day by day. Write a sentence to the Lord, either your own lament or another kind of prayer based on today's scriptures, starting with the letter C.

Christ is my firm foundation

DAY 4

Jerusalem had no one to comfort her.
LAMENTATIONS 1:12–17*

When we're suffering, it can feel like our emotional experience is completely unique — like no one in the world has ever carried the weight we're carrying. We feel stranded on an island that doesn't even show up on anyone else's map.

In Lamentations 1:12, Jerusalem voices this isolating grief: *"Look and see if there is any sorrow like my sorrow ..."* Ironically, we can probably all relate to this sense that no one can relate to our pain.

- In Lamentations 1:16, what does Jerusalem say *"is far from me"*? In verse 17, *"there is none to"* do what?

  The comforter, who restores life. There is no one to comfort.

Another book of the Bible where we see profound suffering is Job, which tells the story of a righteous man whom Satan tormented. Job had a few friends who visited him when he was at his lowest, but their words were cruel, not comforting.

- Read Job 19:21. What did Job appeal to his friends for?

  He was asking his friends to have pity on him.

It is in our nature to want to be surrounded by others when hard times are upon us — and the comfort of close friends and family is truly a blessing from the Lord. But of course, there is no substitute for comfort straight from the Lord Himself. Let's notice a small detail found in Lamentations 1:17. It says, *"Zion stretches out her hands ..."* Her hands stretched outward to other people for comfort. She tried reaching for *"neighbors"* who were instead enemies, desperate for anyone to hold on to. But maybe instead of only looking **out**, she could have first looked **up**.

- Read 2 Corinthians 1:3-5. Who can we look to first for comfort in our affliction? Also important, what do we then do with that comfort?

  Jesus —

  We are then able to comfort others

WEEK 1 | 29

The ultimate comforter is God. We should first seek comfort in Him. But God also doesn't desire for us to feel like an island all alone. He wants us to be there for others who are reaching out, that we might point them back to Him.

- Are you feeling alone along a hard road you are facing? If so, write a prayer asking God to be your source of comfort and strength.

> God, sometimes I feel like I am misunderstood. Especially by my friends like I am the only one who cares or tries. Please help me to not feel alone & show me that you are the only approval I need.

- Next, ask God to show you how you can be a comfort to someone else today. In what way can you point them toward Jesus?

> God show me how to give your comfort to others. Let it ooze out of me & people feel your love.

BIBLICAL HIGHLIGHT:

Lamentations 1:14 says Jerusalem's "transgressions were bound into a yoke." A yoke is a wooden beam that goes across the necks of animals to attach them to a cart or plow. The yoke of our sins is a hard and heavy weight to carry. However, today, we can trade that for the yoke of Christ. Jesus said, "My yoke is easy, and my burden is light" (Matthew 11:30).

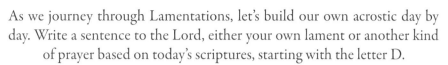

D

As we journey through Lamentations, let's build our own acrostic day by day. Write a sentence to the Lord, either your own lament or another kind of prayer based on today's scriptures, starting with the letter D.

Design a new way for me to comfort others just like you comfort me.

DAY 5

Jerusalem acknowledged that God was right in His judgment.

In reading Lamentations, it can sometimes start to feel like Jerusalem was blaming God for all the suffering she endured. However, in today's verses, we catch a glimpse of a truth that all of us can be quick to forget.

- According to Lamentations 1:18, because Jerusalem had rebelled against His Word, was the Lord right or wrong in afflicting the people?

BIBLICAL HIGHLIGHT:

Lamentations 1:18 says, "Hear, all you peoples, and see my suffering …" Just because we know the Truth of God and His goodness and righteousness does not mean that our pain will suddenly be whisked away every time we suffer. It is OK, in some moments, to know God is good even though we may not feel good at the time.

It is easy for us to read the descriptions of captivity and starvation in today's reading and think, *Wow, that seems so extreme. Was that really necessary just because they disobeyed God?* But this is because it's also easy for us to forget what sin really is. Sin encompasses all the ways we fall short of God's glory in our thoughts, actions, words and attitudes — but there's more to it than just falling short or missing the mark. Theologian R.C. Sproul writes, "If we take the reality of sin seriously in our lives, we see that we commit crimes against a holy God and against His kingdom … any transgression [against] a holy God is vicious by definition."[1]

- Let's remind ourselves of what the Bible says about sin. According to Romans 3:23, who has sinned and rebelled against God? And according to Romans 6:23, what is the price of that sin?

  Death   all have sinned.

Sometimes we fall into the trap of thinking good things always happen to good people and bad things always happen to bad people — and we count ourselves among the "good" as long as we try our best to be helpful and kind and nice. Sure, we mess up sometimes, but we think nothing really bad should happen to us, almost as if God "owes" us. However, this philosophy (similar to the idea of karma) isn't biblical. In fact, nothing could be further from the truth. The truth is that we are all sinners.

- Read Psalm 51:4. What words does David say here that are similar to the words we read in Lamentations 1:18?

  That he rebelled or sinned against Gods commandments

What happened to Israel and Judah in 586 B.C. is a very real reminder that sin has consequences and that God keeps His word. And if the Bible stopped here, it would be true and just ... but utterly hopeless. *THANK YOU, Lord Jesus, that the story doesn't end there!*

- Continue reading Psalm 51, this time picking up in verses 7-12. What is the mood of these verses? What brought the psalmist hope?

  yearning for God, wanting restoration. Hope = faith in God.

God owes us nothing. We are sinners deserving of punishment. But today, we know He sent Jesus to take away our sin, wash us whiter than snow, and return to us **joy** and **life** — and this is an incomparable gift.

- What immeasurable love! What beautiful grace! Take a moment to thank God for every good and precious gift in your life.

E

As we journey through Lamentations, let's build our own acrostic day by day. Write a sentence to the Lord, either your own lament or another kind of prayer based on today's scriptures, starting with the letter E.

WEEKEND REFLECTION
& PRAYER *Week 1*

In these first verses of Lamentations, we've already seen God's people processing a number of emotions, many of which we might relate to in our own lives. And let's be honest — in the midst of hard feelings, we often turn to the world for comfort. It might look like food, fun or other pleasures to numb us from the pain. It might look like reaching out to people with overinflated expectations that they can completely comfort and understand us. But all of these idols will fail in time. Sin has left this world in a painful mess.

But oh, what a God we have, that He would send Jesus to take all of our sin and shame with Him to the cross, crucifying it there, covering it with His blood. Because of Christ, we have found our source of comfort. It is Him. It is knowing that He reigns over sin and death. He sees every feeling and thought we have, and He is waiting with open arms for us to come to Him.

Let's use words from Lamentations to guide us as we pray.

> *Oh, Lord, our God, we come to You in humble prayer today.*
>
> *Lamentations 1:1 says,* "How lonely ..."
>
> [Take a moment to tell the Lord how you are feeling about a particular hard situation in your life.]
>
> *Lamentations 1:9 says,* "She took no thought of her future ..."
>
> [Ask God to help you fix your mind on eternal things above (Colossians 3:2).]
>
> *Lamentations 1:16 says,* "A comforter is far from me ..."
>
> [Pray that God would make you fully aware of the Comforter and Helper, the Holy Spirit, alive and at work within you (John 14:26).]
>
> *Thank You, Lord God, that I can come to You in honesty with everything I am feeling today. I trust in You for both Your Truth and Your comfort today.*
>
> *In Jesus' name, amen.*

Notes

Notes

WEEK

Two

DAY 6

Last week we talked about emotions of hurt, sadness, shame and loneliness. Today, let's take a look at another emotion expressed in Lamentations.

- Starting with the last line of Lamentations 1:21 and reading through verse 22, what emotions do you think are present in these lines? What did Jerusalem want to happen?

  jealousy?   Jerusalem wanted Justice
  bitterness

Somewhere along the journey of a painful situation, we will often experience anger. That anger is usually directed toward the thing we see as the cause of our pain, whether that be a person, a group of people, a disease or any number of circumstances.

- The prophet Jeremiah lived through many of the events Lamentations is referring to. So let's read Jeremiah 11:20. What did Jeremiah ask for from the Lord here?

  Jeremiah asks to see the Lords vengeance
  on Jerusalem

- Before we leave this verse, let's break it down a bit. The first two lines remind us the Lord judges **righteously** because He alone knows and tests what? And at the end of this verse, Jeremiah put the "*cause*" and the need for vengeance into whose hands?

  - minds
  into the Lords hands

BIBLICAL HIGHLIGHT:

Lamentations 1:20 says, "I am in distress; my stomach churns ..."
Jeremiah 4:19 says, "Oh the walls of my heart! My heart is beating wildly ..." We should be mindful of the very real physical effects of painful emotions.

Feelings of anger and vengeance are a normal part of being human. This is not to say it's OK for us to walk around fussing and fuming every day — we should confess and repent of our *unrighteous anger* and the other sins it often holds hands with, like bitterness, pride and jealousy. Yet because we are made in the image of God, we all have a sense of God's justice inside of us that moves us to *righteous anger* in the face of evil. Justice demands that evil does not go unpunished.

- Read Revelation 20:11-15. What will God do to evil someday? And as a reminder, after this event takes place, what will go away, according to Revelation 21:4?

all evil will be cast to the lake of fire.

There will be no more death, sadness, tears, no pain.

There is a subtle yet poignant line in Lamentations 1:22, which says, "*Deal with them as you have dealt with me because of all my transgressions.*" Jerusalem's plea to the Lord to deal with Babylon was not self-justification or some kind of unbalanced comparison. Jerusalem recognized she was not innocent of sin and evil herself.

- Why might this be important to remember in our anger?

in anger, we say things we don't mean & point fingers like we are never wrong

Because we know God has a plan to punish evil and we remember the fact that we ourselves are not perfect, we can then take the position of Romans 12:19, which says, *"Beloved, never avenge yourselves, but leave it to the wrath of God, for it is written, 'Vengeance is mine, I will repay, says the Lord.'"* This is the position Jerusalem seems to have taken in Lamentations 1:20-22: The people had a right to be angry about the evils of Babylon and to express that righteous anger to God, but they ultimately recognized it was God's job to *"deal with"* their enemies. Only God can rightly do so.

God is the only judge & jury.

- Take a moment to express to God any anger you might be feeling today. Confess to the Lord any vengeful thoughts that have been sitting in your mind. Know that the Lord understands your pain, and trust that He will judge righteously in the end. Leave it in His hands.

I am angry that things take so long & that I am fraid to be patient. I am not sure I feel vengeance.

F

As we journey through Lamentations, let's build our own acrostic day by day. Write a sentence to the Lord, either your own lament or another kind of prayer based on today's scriptures, starting with the letter F.

Find me grateful, Find me Faithful. Find me on my knees.

DAY 7

Let's be honest: Today's section of Scripture feels hard when we first read through it. However, the truth tucked inside these verses is powerful and moving. Let's dig in by going straight to the heart of one of the most difficult verses. Lamentations 2:2 says, "*The Lord has swallowed up **without mercy**"* (emphasis added). In Hebrew, this verse uses the word *hamal*, which can also be translated "*without pity*" (NIV) or "*has not spared*" (AMP).

- Before we jump in, take a moment to read today's verses a couple of times. Jot down what feelings these verses provoke in you.

*Devouring
fury
swallowed up*

withdrawn his protection

To fully understand what verse 2 means, let's put this verse into the context of the Bible as a whole. Deuteronomy 4:31 says, "*The LORD your God is a merciful God. He will not leave you or destroy you or forget the covenant with your fathers that he swore to them.*" Part of this covenant between God and His people included very severe consequences if they were to break it. And break the covenant they did. The people rebelled over ... and over ... and over again.

- Read 2 Chronicles 36:15-17. Because our merciful God had compassion on His people, what did He "*persistently*" send? And what was the reaction of the people? Therefore, what eventually happened?

messages / warnings, but they mocked him, so the king of the Chaldeans killed them - no compassion

Lamentations 2:5 mentions "mourning and lamentation." *Bible scholar Hetty Lalleman points out that the two Hebrew words translated as* "mourning" *and* "lamentation" *are similar and even sound like a lament when spoken (much like our* "oohs" *and* "aahs").*[1]

Verse 5 also says, "The Lord has become like an enemy." *What a reminder that we cannot be neutral about God. We either worship and trust Him as our Lord and Savior (making sin and Satan our enemies), or we worship and trust sinful idols (making God our enemy).*

When Lamentations 2:2 says God acted *"without mercy,"* it is saying that while our God is a good and merciful God, He is also a perfect Judge. This verse doesn't imply that God's character changed or that He ran out of mercy; it means His discipline of Jerusalem aligned with His character of perfect justice. God Himself is still merciful even when He withholds His mercy. God's mercy is His prerogative to give generously when He desires. And here we see God withholding mercy to show justice.

- According to Acts 17:31, the Lord has fixed a day on which to do what?

  Judge the world in rightousness

- On that day, we will all appear before the judgment seat so that we might do what, according to 2 Corinthians 5:10?

  receive the things dan in body
  Recene our judgment.

When God doesn't x
do what you
say. @ it's
Protection

On Day 5, we walked through the truth that we are all sinners. To be judged according to our acts would bring us punishment. Yet thankfully, Jesus took on the punishment we deserved. He bore the wrath of God on our behalf. Talk about a merciful God!

- Read Lamentations 2:1-5 again. This time, look at these words of God's destruction and anger as being directed toward Jesus when He hung on the cross, carrying our sin and shame. In what ways does that change your view of this reading?

As we journey through Lamentations, let's build our own acrostic day by day. Write a sentence to the Lord, either your own lament or another kind of prayer based on today's scriptures, starting with the letter G.

DAY 8

Lamentations 2:6-10 is a continuation of the sentiments in yesterday's reading. It is a lament of the devastation that the Lord allowed to happen to Jerusalem as a result of their sin. In particular, verses 6-7 lament the destruction of the Lord's sanctuary and altar. We find similar phrasing in the words of Psalm 74.

• Read Psalm 74:3-8 and take note of the similarities. Then read Psalm 74:9. What is the final line of this verse (*"and there is …"*)? When have you felt the same way in your own life? — destroying.   destruction.

not having life go the way you thought it would.

Temple worship was a big part of life in Old Testament times. The temple was more than a building: It was where people made sacrifices for their sins and gave offerings to God in praise. The priests in the temple were intercessors who communicated between God and His people. And the Ark of the Covenant, a holy vessel that contained the Ten Commandments God had given Israel, was like God's throne on earth (called a "mercy seat"), where God communicated with the high priest (Exodus 25:17-22; 1 Samuel 4:4). This was a huge part of Israel's connection to God. Without the temple, they felt like they had lost their bond and their contact with the Lord.

• The psalmist in Psalm 74:1 cried, *"O God, why do you cast us off forever?"* Why do you think hard times make us feel distant from the Lord?

Because we expect God to always do good for us.

• Yet what truth are we reminded of in Isaiah 57:15?

God restores & revives

While the words of Isaiah 57:15 are a comfort, it is important to point out one specific caveat of this promise of God's presence: God is with those *"who [are] of a contrite and lowly spirit."* It is not that God moves away or becomes distant from us in our pride and unrepentance, but we can move away from Him. To have a contrite and lowly spirit is to humbly turn away from our sin and toward God. Our repentance draws us near to our Father. Part of why the people in Lamentations felt so far from God is that they had pulled themselves away and lacked humble hearts of repentance for what they had done.

In Lamentations 2:8, the Lord *"stretched out the measuring line"* to destroy the walls of Jerusalem. A measuring line was typically used for careful and precise construction, yet here the image is of careful and precise **destruction**. God's plan in the destruction was precisely that — a carefully thought-out plan.

- Read Jeremiah 18:11-12. Was God's plan a secret? Did God spring this plan on His people suddenly? Who else in these verses had a plan, and why was that a problem?

> NO it wasn't. He made it clear.
> The people had a plan to
> live stubbornly & how
> they wanted

Lamentations 2:8 says, "The LORD determined to lay in ruins the wall ..." The walls built around ancient cities were their protection. A strong wall made them feel safe. But God broke down Jerusalem's wall to show that while they thought they were safe from invaders, the true enemy — sin — had captured their hearts. Sometimes the Lord breaks down the walls we have put around our hearts as well. It can feel vulnerable, but it reminds us our true safety is in Him!

Some days on this earth feel like an eternity, especially when they are hard. Especially when God feels distant. Yet it is important to remember that God always has a good plan. And His good plan will always prevail.

- What are we reminded of in Job 42:2?

God can do anything
well No one can stop him!

Praise

- And what does God's purpose look like in 1 John 3:1-2?

To be like him
To strive to be like him
pure

God's purpose = God's plan

H

As we journey through Lamentations, let's build our own acrostic day by day. Write a sentence to the Lord, either your own lament or another kind of prayer based on today's scriptures, starting with the letter H.

DAY 9

Before we begin today, let's put before our eyes the faces of who we will be discussing.

* Think of the children you know in your life. Are any of them facing loss, disease, pain or other heavy circumstances? Maybe it is your own child, the child of a friend or church member, or even a face on the news or in your neighborhood grocery store. Write down some of the hard circumstances facing children today.

down syndrome
- walker braces on legs, glasses

Seeing a child suffering is heart-wrenching. No matter the circumstances, it seems unfair to see children in pain. The poet of Lamentations would agree.

* Lamentations 2:11 describes a person whose "*eyes are spent with weeping*" and whose stomach will not stop twisting because they are mourning who?

Jerusalem

* Verse 12 says: "*They cry to their mothers, 'Where is bread and wine?'*" It also says they "*faint like a wounded man*" and "*their life is poured out.*" This is metaphorical language, but if you had to describe this scene literally, what was going on?

We know and can understand on a certain level why Israel's sin had led to their destruction. However, it becomes so much more difficult when we see that innocent children also suffered the consequences.

The truth is that the vulnerable and small are affected by this sin-shattered world we live in, just like everyone else. Seeing this causes our hearts and stomachs to ache much like the poet's in Lamentations — and it should. We should feel indignation toward the suffering of little ones and toward the sin that causes this world to be so broken. And we should remember that these sufferings upset our Father God even more than they upset us. God Himself lovingly forms each child in the womb (Psalm 139:13-16). Pain across generations is **not** what God ever wanted for His people. But devastatingly, in the same way that all of us today are children of Adam and Eve who suffer the consequences of the very first sin they committed in the garden of Eden (Genesis 3), the children of the Israelites suffered the effects of their parents' sins.

BIBLICAL HIGHLIGHT:

Lamentations 2:14 says, "Your prophets have seen for you false and deceptive visions." These false prophets often told the people what they wanted to hear, which was only good news. They told the people that everything they did was right and fine — even when it was actually sinful. Do we have people in our lives who will tell us the hard truth when we need it even if it hurts? If so, let's cherish those friends! If not, let's pray for God to bring such people into our lives.

- Because we are created in the image of our Creator, the ways that sin hurts our fellow image bearers should break our hearts. In response, what commands does the Lord give us in Isaiah 1:17?

- Defend orphans
  Stand up for widows

- Take some time today to lament, pray and call out to God on behalf of any hurting child, anyone oppressed, any lonely soul or anyone facing injustice today. Write your prayer below:

God I thankyou for your Grace upon Grace. Please help us to show love to those hurting. Protect our children from the sin of this world. Protect their innocence.

I

As we journey through Lamentations, let's build our own acrostic day by day. Write a sentence to the Lord, either your own lament or another kind of prayer based on today's scriptures, starting with the letter I.

DAY 10

Though God had allowed the destruction,
God was also the only One who could save.
LAMENTATIONS 2:15–19

Today's reading begins with the enemies of Israel gloating. According to Lamentations 2:16, the enemies cried, *"We have swallowed [Jerusalem]!"* Yet this was not entirely true, and the poet was quick to say so: The enemies of God's people tried to take the credit for their defeat, but they weren't actually the ones in charge.

• Specifically, according to verse 17, what did the Lord carry out?

> He carried out his promise that
> he would destroy Jerusalem

Remember: Long before Babylon was an empire, God had entered into a covenant with His people. Leviticus 26 and Deuteronomy 28 record the extraordinary blessings for keeping the covenant as well as the consequences for breaking the covenant. For hundreds of years, God not only faithfully upheld His side of the covenant, but also, when the people turned away from Him, He sent warnings and prophets to help them obey. Yet the people refused to listen (2 Kings 17:7-23). Because God is good and faithful and never ever breaks a promise, His word was carried out, as Lamentations says.

• While it is hard to watch Jerusalem go through pain, why is it also comforting to know God's word always gets carried out?

> He won't ever
> fail me.
> I can stand on his promises

Yes, God had allowed the destruction. And while that hurts, in today's reading, the poet also set up an answer to the question posed in Lamentations 2:13: *"Who can heal [Jerusalem]?"*

• In verses 18-19, who did the poet suggest they could cry out to?

> Cry out a pour hearts out
> to the Lord

The One who allowed destruction was also the only One who could save them. Lamentations 2:19 says, *"Pour out your heart like water before the presence of the Lord"* — what a beautiful image of our tears before God. And it's worth noting that the poet didn't just describe tears falling from the people's eyes; this was a soul-deep weeping of the **heart**. The poet was calling God's people to do more than just feel sad about their circumstances or even their sin. He was calling them to truly repent and receive His forgiveness, restoration and healing.

- According to Matthew 10:28, who alone should we fear, and why? Acts 4:11-12 says who alone can offer us salvation?

    God - he can destroy both soul & body   Jesus

Sometimes in our pain, we feel mad at God. We don't understand His ways, and it hurts. And yet ... the deeper the roots of our faith grow, we find ourselves crying out to Him all the more because we know that no one and nothing else can help us.

- Read the exchange between Peter and Jesus in John 6:66-68. How do Peter's words reflect a similar sentiment? How can you make them your words today too?

    He was basically saying there is no one else to go to other than God - so why would they leave?

J

As we journey through Lamentations, let's build our own acrostic day by day. Write a sentence to the Lord, either your own lament or another kind of prayer based on today's scriptures, starting with the letter J.

WEEKEND REFLECTION & PRAYER *Week 2*

The feelings we explored through Lamentations this week were sometimes dark and heavy. And let's be honest: On a very real level, we understand. We know what it is like to feel angry. We sometimes wonder where God is and why He won't extend mercy when our pain is so very obvious. We hurt when we see innocent children having to wade through the ugliest parts of life on earth. Yet even in all of these dark emotions, we also saw the truth that God is always both merciful and just. We refreshed our minds with the reminder that God is never far from us, always waiting with open arms. We recollected that God keeps His promises forever and that He is the only One who can mend and heal our broken hearts.

With this in mind, let's use verses from Lamentations to guide our prayer this weekend.

Lord, Father God,

Today we bow before Your throne in prayer. In the words of Lamentations 1:20, "Look, O LORD, for I am in distress ..."

[Bring before the Lord all that troubles you today. Set down your cares at His feet.]

Lamentations 2:13 asks, "Who can heal you?" In answer to this verse, I pray the words of Jeremiah 17:14: "Heal me, O LORD, and I shall be healed; save me, and I shall be saved, for you are my praise."

Lamentations 2:17 says You "carried out [Your] word, which [You] commanded long ago." Thank You, God, for always being true to Your word. Please carry out Your word once again in fulfillment of the final words of the Bible: "He who testifies to these things says, 'Surely I am coming soon.' Amen. Come, Lord Jesus!" (Revelation 22:20).

Thank You, Lord God, that Your Word is true. See us today in our troubles and pain. Heal us as only You can. We wait in hopeful expectation of a perfect eternity with You.

In Jesus' name, amen.

Notes

Notes

WEEK

Three

DAY 11

Jerusalem questioned God.
LAMENTATIONS 2:20-22

In Lamentations 2:19b, the poet told Jerusalem to *"pour out your heart like water before the presence of the Lord!"* And so, in today's reading, she did just that. However, what we find here is not a tidy, pretty little moment. It is an outpouring of honest, messy emotion.

- In Lamentations 2:20, what are the three questions Jerusalem asked of God?

These are heavy questions. Jerusalem was basically asking, *God, are You actually good, and do You even care?* While we may be somewhat shocked at the boldness of these questions, there is another part of us that probably understands. When we look at the suffering in our world — disasters, wars, loss, sickness, brokenness — the answers to Jerusalem's "should" questions in verse 20 seems clear: *No, this should not be happening.*

And that's ultimately God's answer too. While it's true that Jerusalem was righteously judged by God in Lamentations, the way the world **should** be, as God lovingly created it, is *"very good"* (Genesis 1:31). But since sin entered God's good world (Genesis 3), we face a lot of confusing and painful situations; some we create through our own bad choices, and others we get swept up in by no fault of our own. And in these situations, God doesn't ask us to pretend like we don't have questions.

- What big questions have you had about God, either in the past or still today?

- First Peter 5:7 says, *"Casting all your anxieties on him, because he cares for you."* Why might it be healing to know that you can honestly bring your deepest, darkest thoughts and feelings openly before God and He will listen and not leave you?

The poet of Lamentations didn't shy away from the ugly. Cannibalism and slaughter are graphic images of the reality in Jerusalem many years ago (Lamentations 2:20-21). This wasn't just an ordinary storm of life — this was a hurricane. It was extreme in ways most of us will hopefully never experience and can hardly imagine.

But even if our own experiences are not as extreme today, we all know that life has a way of testing the strength of our spiritual, mental and emotional foundations. And when that happens, we can honestly bring our questions and ugly realities to our God. God's Truth will hold. Our foundation may feel like it's cracking under pressure, but as long as we build our lives on Him, God promises that we will be *"able to withstand in the evil day, and having done all, to stand firm"* (Ephesians 6:13). He will hold us fast. In fact, two of the best questions we can ever ask to strengthen our foundation are found in Psalm 18:31: *"For who is God, but the LORD? And who is a rock, except our God?"*

- Read Matthew 7:24-27. What can life's storms show us? How do you build your faith on the Rock of Christ?

As we journey through Lamentations, let's build our own acrostic day by day. Write a sentence to the Lord, either your own lament or another kind of prayer based on today's scriptures, starting with the letter K.

DAY 12

A firsthand witness felt trapped by God.
LAMENTATIONS 3:1-9

So far in Lamentations, the poet and Jerusalem are the only two characters who have spoken. In Chapter 3, we have a change in speaker. Now *"the man who has seen affliction"* (Lamentations 3:1) steps up to deliver his firsthand account of what happened. Eventually he will deliver some words of hope — but not before he expresses what he felt through the devastation.

• As we think about processing our emotions in a biblical way, why is it important that we see this witness work through his grief first instead of just swooping in with a hopeful, cheery attitude right away? Have you ever tried to "skip over" grief to get to hope, and if so, what was the result?

Powerfully evident throughout today's reading is this foundational truth: Sometimes there is a difference between what we *feel* to be the truth and what *is* the truth according to God's Word.

• Let's break down the speaker's feelings in today's verses and fill in the chart below as we go:

IMAGES IN SCRIPTURE	WHAT DID THE MAN FEEL IN LAMENTATIONS FEEL?	WHAT DO OTHER SCRIPTURES SAY?
God's Rod	Lamentations 3:1	Psalm 23:4; Proverbs 13:24

WEEK 3 | 59

IMAGES IN SCRIPTURE	WHAT DID THE MAN IN LAMENTATIONS FEEL?	WHAT DO OTHER SCRIPTURES SAY?
God's Hand	Lamentations 3:3	Isaiah 41:10; Deuteronomy 11:2
Darkness	Lamentations 3:6	1 Peter 2:9; Ephesians 5:11
Prison and Chains	Lamentations 3:7-8	Psalm 107:10-16
Paths	Lamentations 3:9	Proverbs 3:6; Psalm 25:10

The man in Lamentations 3 felt the heavy chains of his sin and its consequences — but his feelings prevented him from seeing that God is also a Chain Breaker for His people. The man was plunged into the darkness of sin and suffering — but in his despair, he failed to see God calling him into "*marvelous light*" (1 Peter 2:9). It's not that the man's feelings were *wrong* (at least, not in all cases), but they were based on a clouded view of God's character and His actions.

Lamentations 3:3 says, "Surely against me he turns his hand again and again the whole day long." *In Scripture, God's hand is often used as a metaphor for His rescuing power, but here we see God's hand of discipline, which is also described in verses like Psalm 32:4.*

In the end, today's scriptures remind us that sometimes there is a gap between what we feel and the larger reality of what God is doing and who He is. But Truth doesn't change based on how we feel about it. And sometimes we may even need to boss our emotions around with the facts of God's Word.

• What feelings have you had lately that are sitting uncomfortably with you? Do they align with the Truth of God's Word? Consider looking up the verses provided if you need a biblical perspective for these emotions.

FEAR: 2 Timothy 1:7.

LONELINESS: Deuteronomy 31:8.

ANGER: Ephesians 4:26.

ENVY: Proverbs 14:30.

SADNESS: Psalm 34:18.

DOUBT: Proverbs 3:5.

GUILT: 1 John 1:9.

GRIEF: Matthew 5:4.

SHAME: Romans 8:1.

JEALOUSY: James 3:16-17.

ANXIETY: 1 Peter 5:7.

L

As we journey through Lamentations, let's build our own acrostic day by day. Write a sentence to the Lord, either your own lament or another kind of prayer based on today's scriptures, starting with the letter L.

DAY 13

Pastor Tony Evans once said: "Sometimes God lets you hit rock bottom so that you can discover He is the Rock at the bottom." [1] This is a little bit of what we see in Lamentations 3. The speaker, or more accurately, the entire book, reaches rock bottom in this section. Tomorrow, we will discover the true Rock the speaker found there. But for today, Lamentations shows us what it looks like at the lowest point.

• Call to mind one of the lowest points you have experienced in your life. What were the feelings or emotions you had surrounding this moment?

• According to Lamentations 3:18, what two things did the man say had perished, and why?

Few things describe the low points of life better than the man has described it here. In Lamentations 3:13, the speaker said God "*drove into [his] kidneys the arrows of his quiver,*" which may sound a bit strange to us today since we often think of our feelings as coming from our hearts or minds, but in ancient times, the kidneys were considered the seat of emotions. The only other place in Scripture where the word "kidney" is used (outside the context of animal sacrifice) is in Job 16:13, where Job said something similar in the depths of his suffering: "*[God] slashes open my kidneys and does not spare; he pours out my gall on the ground.*"

This is similar to the modern idea of a "knife to the heart": an image that encompasses extreme physical, emotional and even spiritual pain. When we experience this kind of deep wounding, we may be tempted to lose hope.

• What does Proverbs 13:12 say about hope?

In Lamentations 3:20, the man said he "*continually remember[ed]*" his suffering. When we are in a low, dark place, it can be so, so difficult to remember anything other than the pain and loss that surround us. It can be hard to remember there is hope. But as followers of Jesus, we always, always, always have the "*hope of the glory of God*" (Romans 5:2).

• Read Romans 5:2-5. According to verse 3 of this passage, what can we "*rejoice in,*" ultimately producing hope? And why does hope not put us to shame?

Today, let's end with this prayer from Ephesians 1:18: "*I pray that the eyes of your heart may be enlightened in order that you may know the hope to which [God] has called you ...*" (NIV).

• Below, write a prayer based on Ephesians 1:18 to pray over yourself, over your loved ones, and over anyone you know who may be going through a low time and need to be reminded of hope.

As we journey through Lamentations, let's build our own acrostic day by day. Write a sentence to the Lord, either your own lament or another kind of prayer based on today's scriptures, starting with the letter M.

DAY 14

The speaker called to mind the steadfast love of the Lord.
LAMENTATIONS 3:21-24

Remember how we talked about the book of Lamentations being written in chiastic structure at the beginning of this study guide? (See "Poetic Structure of Lamentations" on page 12 if you need a refresher.) Well, today, we have reached the middle. This is the most important part of the book. This is the big point!

But first, let's do a quick recall of yesterday's study.

- In Lamentations 3:18, the narrator said what had perished? And in verse 20, he said that his soul did what?

Yesterday we talked about how dark it is when we reach rock bottom. Now we will see the man in Lamentations make a choice at this turning point ...

- The man's situation felt dark and hopeless. But he did something important in Lamentations 3:21. He said: "**But *this I* _____ *to* _____ ...**" (emphasis added).

I love Dr. Christopher Wright's description of this verse. He says, "It is the deliberate, determined, teeth-gritting decision to call something to mind."[1] This wasn't a reaction based purely on feelings — this was an action of will.

- Let's take action in the same way today. Before we go on, write a prayer to the Lord saying that no matter what you are feeling today, you are determined to stop and truly think on His Truth.

Now, let's soak in the words of Lamentations 3:22-24.

- Write down the truths you find in these verses and what they mean to you. What do they teach you about God?

- What do they teach you about the way God's people can process their emotions compared to those who do not know Him? Read 2 Corinthians 7:10-11, and consider how "*godly grief*" is different from "*worldly grief*."

Lamentations 3:23 says God's mercies "*are new every morning.*" This refers not only to a literal morning but a figurative one as well. Every night, we go to bed knowing that the sun will rise the next day. Morning *will* come. The same is true of God's love and mercy. Even when it feels dark, the daylight of God's illuminating grace and hope is on its way.

If you haven't already, we highly encourage you to memorize Lamentations 3:22-24. (There are a number of resources, like Bible memorizing apps, that can assist you!) Psalm 119:11 says, "*I have stored up your word in my heart, that I might not sin against you.*" The best way to help us "*call to mind*" (Lamentations 3:21) the Truth of God's Word in hard times is to store it in our memories today.

- What is one technique that helps you memorize Scripture? How can you use it with today's verses?

N

As we journey through Lamentations, let's build our own acrostic day by day. Write a sentence to the Lord, either your own lament or another kind of prayer based on today's scriptures, starting with the letter N.

LAMENTATIONS: CHIASTIC STRUCTURE
Outlined[1]

A   Jerusalem desolate *(Lamentations 1:1-11)*

   B   Jerusalem betrayed *(Lamentations 1:12-22)*

     C   The Lord's wrath did this *(Lamentations 2:1-8)*

       D   All suffer, from princes to infants *(Lamentations 2:9-12)*

         E   Cry out to God *(Lamentations 2:13-22)*

           F   The Lord afflicts in mercy *(Lamentations 3:1-20)*

             G   **The Lord's great love and faithfulness (Lamentations 3:21-32)**

           F   The Lord afflicts in mercy *(Lamentations 3:33-39)*

         E   Cry out to God *(Lamentations 3:40-66)*

       D   All suffer, from princes to infants *(Lamentations 4:1-10)*

     C   The Lord's wrath did this *(Lamentations 4:11-16)*

   B   Jerusalem betrayed *(Lamentations 4:17-22)*

A   Jerusalem desolate *(Lamentations 5:1-22)*

DAY 15

The speaker said it is good to wait on God's salvation.
LAMENTATIONS 3:25–30

We started this week talking about how Jerusalem had questioned God's goodness. We were then introduced to a man who talked honestly about the raw pain he felt during this devastating time. But just when he felt more hopeless than he ever thought possible, he deliberately turned his mind to the truth of God's faithfulness.

- Let's pick up in Lamentations 3:25-30. What word is repeated at the beginning of verses 25, 26 and 27?

Interestingly, modern science has shown that repeating a message at least three times can improve our ability to remember and recall the information as well as help our brain accept the message as truth.

- Today, in the space below, write a truth about the Lord that you need to soak into your heart and mind. Then write it at least two more times on notecards or sticky notes, and consider placing those reminders in various places where you will see them this coming week.

Lamentations 3:26 suggests that "*one should wait quietly*" on the Lord. Verse 28 says, "*Let him sit alone in silence ...*" But this advice is coming from the man who just spent 20-something verses verbally lamenting his situation. And spoiler alert — he wasn't done lamenting yet. So was the speaker now saying that his previous outcry of anguish was wrong or uncalled for? Not necessarily. Today's section of verses is a beautiful reminder that we all experience ups and downs, highs and lows, days where we need to scream and cry and days where we sit in silence.

- Read Ecclesiastes 3:1-8. How might this relate to our emotions as well? In what ways is it reassuring to know that the swinging of emotions is normal?

Of course, there is an important difference between allowing ourselves to experience a range of emotions and being emotionally unstable or volatile, getting tossed about by our feelings with every wind of change or circumstance. In the words of Lysa TerKeurst's book *Unglued*, feelings "can indicate where your heart is in the moment, but that doesn't mean they have the right to dictate your behavior and boss you around. You are more than the sum total of your feelings and perfectly capable of that little gift ... called self-control."[1]

Lamentations 3:25-30 talks about waiting for the Lord, which often requires tremendous self-control and surrender to God's plan. For instance, the instruction to "*put [our] mouth in the dust*" (v. 29) teaches us to refrain from grumbling or arguing against God. Having to wait through difficult times can be one of the hardest things to do, but if you find yourself in a season of waiting, you are not alone. Keep holding on, trusting the Lord to come through.

• Read Micah 7:7-8. Turn that verse into your own prayer in the waiting today.

BIBLICAL HIGHLIGHT:

Lamentations 3:30 says, "Let him give his cheek to the one who strikes, and let him be filled with insults." *This verse is very similar to a prophecy about the Messiah that we find in Isaiah 50:6:* "I gave my back to those who strike, and my cheeks to those who pull out the beard; I hid not my face from disgrace and spitting." *It also rings of Jesus' own words,* "But I say to you, Do not resist the one who is evil. But if anyone slaps you on the right cheek, turn to him the other also" *(Matthew 5:39). Jesus is the ultimate example of what it looks like to humbly and patiently walk through difficult times, trusting that God is in control and He will have the victory in the end.*

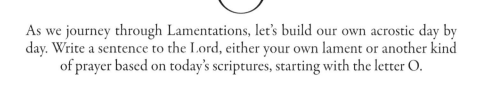

As we journey through Lamentations, let's build our own acrostic day by day. Write a sentence to the Lord, either your own lament or another kind of prayer based on today's scriptures, starting with the letter O.

WEEKEND REFLECTION & PRAYER *Week 3*

This week we looked at questions and feelings that shake people to the core. These faith-shaking moments can be scary. And yet we have also been reminded that God's Truth will always stay firm and God's steadfast love will never cease. Let's be honest: Sometimes we have to forcibly remind ourselves this is true. Sometimes we have to call to mind who God really is. We can't always go by our feelings — or at least, not feelings alone. To plant ourselves on a firm foundation, we need to stand on the Truth of God's Word and the gospel of Jesus. With Christ in mind, we can declare, even in the midst of our pain, that God really is enough.

Let's use verses from Lamentations to guide our prayer.

Lord God most high, today we come before You both in honesty and in humility.

Lamentations 3:1 says, "I am the man who has seen affliction ..."

[Tell the Lord of the afflictions you have seen lately, either in your own life or in the lives of others.]

Yet we declare the faith-filled words of Lamentations 3:24: "'The LORD is my portion,' says my soul, 'therefore I will hope in him.'"

We pray along with the words of Psalm 73:26: "My flesh and my heart may fail, but God is the strength of my heart and my portion forever." We declare that You, Lord, are enough. We ask You to be our portion today.

Lamentations 3:25 says, "The LORD is good ... to the soul who seeks him." Father, we pray that our hearts and minds will seek You today, as Matthew 7:7 says to "seek, and you will find." We anticipate that You will reveal Yourself to us.

Lord Jesus, You are forever enough. Help us to see You today, whatever comes our way.

In Jesus' name, amen.

Notes

Notes

WEEK

Four

DAY 16

"Theology" is just a fancy word for studying the nature of God and developing beliefs based on that study. Today, we are going to research the nature of God and consider what makes for a solid theology that will hold up through anything life brings our way. This is the speaker's point in today's verses. The man in Lamentations is showing us **why** he could talk about waiting for God through suffering — because he knew who God is.

- Lamentations 3:31-33 gives three main truths about God's character. Write them below:

Verse 31	How long does the Lord's punishment (or anger) toward His people endure? (Is it temporary or permanent?)
Verse 32	The Lord "*will have*" what? "*According to*" what?
Verse 33	"*For he does not*" do what?

Look at what you wrote in the chart above. These are true, foundational characteristics about God. Let's look into other scriptures in the Bible to confirm them.

SCRIPTURE	WHAT WE LEARN ABOUT GOD'S CHARACTER
Psalm 103:8	How does this passage describe the Lord?
Isaiah 54:8	What similar things do we learn from the prophet Isaiah about God?
Micah 7:18	And again, what does the prophet Micah say about God?
Hosea 11:8	Though God hates sin and is compelled by His justice to punish it rightfully, what does the thought of punishment do to the heart of God?

The fundamental truth is that God is love (1 John 4:16). His character has always been, and will always be, grounded in compassion and love. That is not to say that God won't sometimes be angry. Deuteronomy 4:24 says, "*For the LORD your God is a consuming fire ...*" God hates sin and evil. But even His wrath is not only wrathful; it is also loving.

Lamentations 3:33 says God "does not afflict from his heart." *The Hebrew word for* "heart" *used here could also be translated as* "wholeheartedly." *In other words, it is not God's desire to see His people commit sins that require punishment. That's why we see throughout Scripture that He offered (and still offers!) many warnings and opportunities to turn toward repentance.*

Psalm 145:17 says, "*The Lord is righteous in* **all** *his ways and kind in* **all** *his works*" (emphases added). He is always — not just sometimes — good and kind. And the best example we have of His kindness is Christ Himself, who sacrificially died for us while we were His enemies (Romans 5:8). Knowing God's love and goodness, we can then trust His promises that all affliction is temporary for those who follow Him. Bible scholar Robin Parry says it this way: "This theology forms the basis for hope in the midst of crisis."[1]

• How does remembering the true, unchanging character of God help you in whatever emotion you are feeling and in whatever situation you are facing?

P

As we journey through Lamentations, let's build our own acrostic day by day. Write a sentence to the Lord, either your own lament or another kind of prayer based on today's scriptures, starting with the letter P.

DAY 17

God seeks justice and is sovereign.
LAMENTATIONS 3:34-39

Today we are going to look into two more fundamental truths about the character of God.

- According to Lamentations 3:34-36, what types of things does the Lord not approve of?

- Read Isaiah 61:8. What does the Lord love?

Justice is defined as behavior and treatment that is morally right and fair. This is who God is. And we like that! We want that of God. In Lamentations, the speaker wanted God to remember justice when it came to what the Babylonians had done to Jerusalem (Lamentations 1:22). He wanted punishment for those who did evil to God's people. And God would remember the Babylonians' crimes — but it's important to know His justice also applies to us, not only to our enemies. The man came to this same conclusion in Lamentations 3:39 when he said, "*Why should a living man complain, a man, about the punishment of his sins?*"

- Have you ever found yourself complaining about a hard circumstance in your life, only to realize that the circumstance was caused or exacerbated by your own wrongdoing? What helped you to realize this? How did you respond?

WEEK 4 | 79

Yes, God is just. And God is also merciful (Deuteronomy 4:31). We might question how these two facts can be true together. And the answer is found perfectly in the life of Christ. Christ is the picture of God's **mercy** in that He took on the **justice** we all deserved.

• Read Romans 5:9-11. For those in Christ, how have we been saved, justified and reconciled?

Death is the justice that evil deserves. Jesus received that justice for all who count on Him for that payment. There is no more beautiful act of mercy than this!

BIBLICAL HIGHLIGHT:

Lamentations 3:35-36 says, "To deny a man justice ... the Lord does not approve." Not only is God Himself characterized by justice, but He expects His people to act justly as well (Micah 6:8).

Lamentations 3:37-39 goes on to confirm another characteristic of God: His sovereignty. According to The Gospel Coalition, "the sovereignty of God is the same as the *lordship* of God, for God is the *sovereign* over all creation ... This rule is exercised through God's authority as king, his control over all things, and his presence with his covenantal people and throughout his creation."[1]

• Look up the following verses. What do these, along with the verses we're studying today in Lamentations, teach us about God's sovereignty?

Psalm 115:3:

Isaiah 45:7:

Job 2:10:

Job 42:2:

Daniel 4:35:

Here is where some honesty hits home. Could God stop all the bad, hard and ugly things in the world? Absolutely. And He will do exactly that in eternity, destroying all evil and gathering His people to live in heaven with Him forever. But does He always prevent or eliminate all evil *now*? No. While evil never comes from God, it is a part of our reality for a time while we live in a fallen world. Still, ultimately nothing can stand against the will of God. And while that truth can be difficult to understand, it is also our hope. God is sovereign, meaning He has all power and authority. And while we might never understand all He does or does not do on this side of heaven, we can have faith that He does know what He is doing.

> BIBLICAL HIGHLIGHT:
>
> "Who has spoken and it came to pass, unless the Lord has commanded it?" *(Lamentations 3:37). These words echo the powerful words of other Bible verses like Psalm 33:9:* "For he spoke, and it came to be; he commanded, and it stood firm." *God's will always prevails.*

- In what ways do God's justice (which promises that all evil will be paid for one way or another) and God's sovereignty (which promises that He is in control) help you walk through whatever you are facing today?

As we journey through Lamentations, let's build our own acrostic day by day. Write a sentence to the Lord, either your own lament or another kind of prayer based on today's scriptures, starting with the letter Q.

DAY 18

So far in Lamentations 3, we've met a man who experienced hardship. Just when he was at his lowest point, the man called to mind the goodness of God. He examined God's character and once again found hope. With that renewed hope, he is now going to encourage others to join him in returning to the Lord.

The first line of Lamentations 3:40 says, "*Let us test and examine our ways.*" Perhaps "*our ways*" refers to our actions, our choices and/or our thoughts. Perhaps it also means our emotions.

- If you were to "*test and examine*" your emotions today, what would you find? A good first step may just be naming some emotions you're feeling. Don't worry if they seem to clash or contradict each other — just write them below. Then take a moment to surrender to God the feelings you've found.

Let's also notice *whose* ways we are told to examine: "***our ways***" (v. 40, emphasis added). We often look at (and assign blame to) other people's ways or emotions when we are upset, but the Bible asks us to focus on our own ways. The only person you and I can control or change is ourselves.

It is also important to remember that feelings provide us with valuable information about what is going on inside us, but they do not have the right to control our behaviors or beliefs. This is another reason why it is so good to test and examine the emotions we have. From there, we can decide if we need to correct our behavior or take action in any way.

For instance, in Lamentations 3:42, the man said, *"We have transgressed and rebelled, and you [God] have not forgiven."* This can seem like a shocking verse since we know God is forgiving in His character — but notice that in this line, and indeed in the entire book thus far, the people had not *asked* God to forgive them. They needed to take action to repent.

- According to the second line of Lamentations 3:40, testing and examining our ways should always lead us back to the Lord. What does 2 Chronicles 15:4 remind us will happen when we turn to the Lord?

No matter what feelings we are experiencing today, we can let them bring us closer to our God. Whether we are happy, sad, angry, peaceful, worried, confused or shocked, we can always *"lift up our hearts and hands to God in heaven"* (Lamentations 3:41). By adding the phrase *"in heaven,"* the writer of Lamentations reminds us that we are here on earth, but God reigns above. God is higher than we are. He is sovereign over all.

BIBLICAL HIGHLIGHT:

Lifting up our hearts is an inward surrender to the Lord. Lifting up our hands is an outward expression. Like faith and works, they complement each other. The work of our hands is an expression of the change in our hearts (James 2:17).

- In what ways can you lift your heart and hands to God in heaven today?

As we journey through Lamentations, let's build our own acrostic day by day. Write a sentence to the Lord, either your own lament or another kind of prayer based on today's scriptures, starting with the letter R.

DAY 19

In the previous verses, we witnessed the unnamed sufferer in Lamentations encouraging himself and others to *"return to the LORD!"* (Lamentations 3:40). For the remainder of Chapter 3, we will see the man eventually did just that. But as he continued to speak to God, what he said first may shock us.

- In reading today's verses, how would you describe the man's feelings? Have you ever spoken to God in this tone? Why or why not?

What a gift it is that God purposefully allowed these hard words to become a part of His holy, inspired Word. The Lord can handle whatever feelings we have. These verses are proof that He wants us to bring everything to Him. We can be completely honest with God.

- Reread today's verses, keeping in mind that God intentionally wanted us to read these words. What do you learn from this?

Just when it seemed like the man was coming to a good place, emotionally speaking, in Lamentations 3:22-41, his anger and pain came bubbling to the surface again starting in verse 43. One thing this reminds us is that healing takes time. It is a slow process, with ups and downs along the way. Neuroscientist Dr. Caroline Leaf states, "It's okay to be fed up with how long it takes. You are not a failure for feeling fed up or frustrated, and this is not a sign you are regressing. Recovery is hard."[1]

- Think of a time when you felt like you had been making progress in processing difficult emotions in your life, only to have the struggle or hurt return. How did you feel at that moment? Or perhaps it is someone else's slow healing you've been frustrated with. Why is it important to remember that healing takes time?

Speaking about a situation where Israel was suffering the consequences of sin, Hosea 6:1 says the Lord "*struck us down, and **he will bind us up**.*" Psalm 147:3 also says the Lord "*heals the brokenhearted and **binds up their wounds***" (emphases added). Whether our heartbreak is an undeserved outcome of others sinning against us or even if it's caused by our own sin, God forgives those who seek His forgiveness. He comforts and mends.

- To bind a wound is to cover it, to wrap it, to give it time to heal. In what ways might God "*bind up*" your wounds?

- Bandaged wounds can still hurt. What can we do to continue trusting God when the pain comes back?

Friends, someday Jesus will return. He will come back in radiant light and glory. And when He does, you will receive what your heart longs for ...

- Read Isaiah 58:8-9a. What will we receive from God one day if we are part of God's family through faith in Christ?

S

As we journey through Lamentations, let's build our own acrostic day by day. Write a sentence to the Lord, either your own lament or another kind of prayer based on today's scriptures, starting with the letter S.

DAY 20

In yesterday's reading, the suffering man, in his pain, spoke as though God were his enemy. In today's reading, there is a shift in perspective. The man moved from seeing God as the enemy to realizing God was his only rescue.

• When we are in the *"depths of the pit"* (Lamentations 3:55), the only way to look for help is up. What did the psalmist say about this in Psalm 121:1-2?

Lamentations 3:49-50 speaks of tears flowing "*without ceasing ... **until** the LORD from heaven looks down and sees*" (emphasis added). These words express an *expectant* waiting. This is faith. It doesn't mean we always have to put on a brave face or that we never grieve or cry as we wait on the Lord — but it means we have hope even as we weep.

The poet's words *"my eyes will flow without ceasing"* (v. 49) echo the words of the prophet Jeremiah when he spoke of Jerusalem, saying, *"Let my eyes run down with tears night and day, and let them not cease"* (Jeremiah 14:17). Today, because we have the blessing of the full revelation of Scripture, including the New Testament, we know there was also another man who would draw near to the city of Jerusalem one day, and when He "*saw the city, he wept over it*" (Luke 19:41). His name? Jesus. His mission? To secure eternal redemption for all who would believe in Him, guaranteeing the end of their weeping forever (Revelation 21:4).

Hebrews 11:1 says "*faith is the assurance of things hoped for, the conviction of things not seen.*" **Faith means expectantly waiting on what we cannot yet see based on what we already know about God.** When life is hard, it is important that we lean on faith. We can expectantly believe that God is present.

- What assurance do we have in Psalm 18:6?

- When God's people cried out for rescue from Egypt, what was God's response in Exodus 2:24-25? What reassurance does that give you today as well?

One of the most encouraging moments from Lamentations is found in today's passage. In this section, we find the only recorded words spoken by God Himself in this book, a response to the man's outcry of repentance and his despairing lament, "*I am lost*" (Lamentations 3:54). And God's powerful statement couldn't be more meaningful.

- Record God's words in verse 57: "*You said, '_____ _____ _____!*'"

- Now write down what God says to you in Isaiah 41:13. In what area of your life do you need to hear these words from the Lord? How does hearing them affect your heart and mind?

- Let's end by taking a step back and getting the big picture of Lamentations 3:55-58. When we call out to God with humble hearts, what can we expect from Him?

In the verse below, we have highlighted the phrases that speak of God's action plan:

"*I called on your name, O L*ORD*, from the depths of the pit;* **you heard** *my plea, 'Do not close your ear to my cry for help!'* **You came near** *when I called on you;* **you said, 'Do not fear!' You have taken up my cause,** *O Lord;* **you have redeemed** *my life*" (Lamentations 3:55-58, emphases added).

Our God hears. Our God comes near. Our God is ready and willing to help.

T

As we journey through Lamentations, let's build our own acrostic day by day. Write a sentence to the Lord, either your own lament or another kind of prayer based on today's scriptures, starting with the letter T.

WEEKEND REFLECTION & PRAYER *Week 4*

We have meditated deeply on the character of God this week. We have seen that God is love and compassion. In love, He also exercises both justice and mercy. He is sovereign over all creation and all time. But let's be honest: Our feelings don't always remember who God is. When healing takes time and pain resurfaces, we have to intentionally and continually do the work of anchoring our hope in exactly who God says He is. We stake our hearts and minds to the truth that God hears, He draws near, and He says, *"Do not fear!"* (Lamentations 3:57).

Let's allow these verses from Lamentations to guide our prayer for this week.

Good and kind Father in heaven, today we bring You our hearts.

Lamentations 3:33 says You "[do] not afflict from [Your] heart." *Our affliction on this earth hurts, Lord — but we praise You that these* "present sufferings are not worth comparing with the glory that will be revealed" *(Romans 8:18, NIV).*

[Bring God your concerns, and see the compassion in His eyes. Hear Him whisper, *This is not the end of the story* ...]

Lamentations 3:41 says, "Let us lift up our hearts and hands to God in heaven." *So we lift our hearts to You in worship. We lift our hands toward heaven. We praise You, God, with everything and for everything.*

Lamentations 3:57 says, "You came near when I called on you." *So we call on the name of Jesus today, knowing and believing that He will come running to be near us (Luke 15:20).*

Gracious Father, thank You that You are always with us. Today, we choose to praise You no matter what else is happening around us. Your goodness and mercy follow us everywhere we go (Psalm 23:6). Yes, Father, **You are good***.*

In Jesus' name, amen.

Notes

Notes

WEEK

Five

DAY 21

The speaker knew God had seen the wrong done to him.

Nothing stirs up our emotions quite like feeling as if we have been wronged. Sometimes emotions like anger, sorrow or indignation are appropriate and even righteous in the face of sinful injustice — but if we're not careful, they may start to transform into something different: bitterness. Bitterness is unresolved anger and resentment. The more we dwell on what has been done to us, the deeper the bitter root grows. Bitterness steals our joy and peace.

- Think of a situation in your life where you allowed (or were tempted to allow) bitterness to take root in your heart. What feelings surrounded that moment? In what ways did those feelings start to affect other areas of your life?

When we read the words of Lamentations 3:59-63, we feel the pain the speaker experienced at the mistreatment from the Babylonians. The taunts, plots and thoughts against him ... This pain was real. This mistreatment was not OK.

- According to Lamentations 3:59, the Lord has *"seen the _____ done to me."* And what will He do in response, according to verse 64?

We might read these verses and think the man was asking for vengeance. And to a degree, he was. But he was also reminding himself (and others) of a very real truth about accountability. It is a truth found not only in the Old Testament but all over the New Testament as well.

- Read Hebrews 4:13 and 2 Corinthians 5:10. What do we learn here?

- Lamentations 3:61-62 says, *"You have heard their taunts, O LORD, all their plots against me. The lips and thoughts of my assailants are against me ..."* It is comforting to know that God even sees the unkind **thoughts** others have against us! What does this also mean about God seeing our own thoughts?

You and I will give an account for our lives one day. So will the people who mistreat us. We are all accountable before God. Lamentations 3:64 says, *"You will repay them, O LORD, according to the work of their hands."* Thankfully, by the grace and blood of Jesus, those who place their faith in Him can stand before the throne and be covered by His righteousness alone, saved by the work of *His hands* outstretched on the cross (Titus 3:5; Philippians 3:9).

So the words of Lamentations 3:64-66, speaking about repaying enemies, cursing them, pursuing them in anger ... Are these words of truth or bitterness? Because Hebrews 12:15 warns us to ensure *"that no 'root of bitterness' springs up and causes trouble, and by it many become defiled,"* how do we guard against bitterness when we are hurt or mistreated?

Perhaps these words in Lamentations are presented as a way to stave off the bitterness that threatens our hearts. Perhaps today's reading prompts us to keep the big picture of eternity in mind. God is on the throne. There is a peace that comes with having no doubt that God will make all things right in the end. Leaving justice in the hands of God is a beautiful way God invites us to experience His redemption in our lives. He takes up our cause (Lamentations 3:58). One day, He will take care of both our pain and the cause of our pain. Trusting Him allows us to leave our roots of bitterness to wither before His throne.

- Read Colossians 3:13, Romans 12:21 and Romans 8:26. What are some other steps that you can take to help uproot bitterness?

U

As we journey through Lamentations, let's build our own acrostic day by day. Write a sentence to the Lord, either your own lament or another kind of prayer based on today's scriptures, starting with the letter U.

DAY 22

As we enter into Chapter 4, we leave behind *"the man who has seen affliction"* (Lamentations 3:1) and his thoughts in Chapter 3. Now the poet picks back up, and in today's reading, the emphasis goes back to the suffering the people of Jerusalem endured. So we've passed the most hopeful part of Lamentations. The rest of the book will be more like the first half. Yet within these words, too, we find valuable lessons.

- Lamentations 4:1 says, *"How the gold has grown dim."* It goes on to say specifically what kind of gold *"changed"*?

Gold is one of the least reactive chemical elements. Because it does not combine easily with oxygen, it does not easily rust, tarnish or corrode ... if it is *pure* gold. Yet verse 1 says the pure gold of Jerusalem had changed and gone dim. In his commentary on Lamentations, Bible scholar Steven Smith says, "The point is simple: the untarnished is now tarnished; what seemed untouchable is now touchable."[1]

- Are there areas of your life that feel "untouchable," like maybe an area in which you think you would never be tempted to sin? Why or why not?

While not pleasant to look at, Lamentations 4 starts out by reminding us that we are all susceptible to sin and the consequences that come with that. The only *"pure gold"* ever to exist was and is Jesus Christ, and any shine we have, we owe to Him.

As we continue through Lamentations 4, the speaker's words become increasingly difficult to hear. We see the people of Jerusalem were once *"worth their weight in fine gold"* (v. 2). They were wealthy (v. 5), handsome and healthy (v. 7). There were even nice or *"compassionate"* (v. 10) people at one time. Yet none of these things could reverse the devastating effects of their sin, which led to death.

Lamentations 4:10 is one of the most difficult verses of all, not only in this book but in the whole Bible. It says, *"The hands of compassionate women have boiled their own children; they became their food ..."* Bible scholar F.B. Huey comments, "The compassion, self-sacrifice, and protectiveness that normally characterize a mother for her children had been replaced by one motive—self-preservation."[2] That mothers would eat their children is arguably the most disturbing, tragic example of how spiritually degraded the people had become.

- How does the outcome of sin contrast against God's law of love, which Jesus described in Matthew 22:37-39? *"You shall love the Lord your God with all your heart and with all your soul and with all your mind. This is the great and first commandment. And a second is like it: You shall love your neighbor as yourself."*

Only God can save us from our sin — not wealth, health, good looks or good works. First Corinthians 15:24-28 tells us that in the end, everything will be subject to God as the King of all. This is exactly why Israel should have been worshipping and obeying Him! God alone is supreme, unchanging, imperishable and truly pure.

- Is there any area in your life where you may be striving for more (wealth, health, appearances, good works, etc.) rather than seeking the Lord? In what ways might your life better reflect worship of God as the only King and Savior?

V

As we journey through Lamentations, let's build our own acrostic day by day. Write a sentence to the Lord, either your own lament or another kind of prayer based on today's scriptures, starting with the letter V.

DAY 23

God's wrath was complete.

Yesterday was a hard look at where sin had taken the people of Israel as they experienced God's wrath. As we finish up Chapter 4, let's take a close look at two particular Hebrew words used to describe God's wrath in today's passage.

The first is found in Lamentations 4:11, which says, "*The LORD gave full vent to his wrath*." The word we translate *"full vent"* in English is the Hebrew word *kalah*. According to the *Bible Sense Lexicon*, *kalah* means "to use up completely."[1] In other words, His wrath came to an end. It was temporary.

Knowing what things are temporary and what things are forever can help give us proper perspective as we walk through life's challenges.

- Let's make a chart to record a small part of what we find in the Bible about what is momentary and what is eternal.

THINGS THAT ARE TEMPORARY FOR GOD'S PEOPLE	THINGS THAT ARE FOREVER
According to Lamentations 4:11, what was vented, or completely used up, and **came to an end**?	According to Lamentations 3:22, what two things **never cease or come to an end**?
According to 2 Corinthians 4:17, what is "*momentary*"?	According to Psalm 107:1 (also repeated many times in Psalm 118 and Psalm 136!), what "*endures forever*"?

102 | WEEK 5

THINGS THAT ARE TEMPORARY FOR GOD'S PEOPLE	THINGS THAT ARE FOREVER
According to 1 Peter 5:10, what will we only have to endure for "*a little while*"?	According to John 3:16, believing in Jesus gives us what that is eternal?

Now let's look at one more Hebrew word from Lamentations 4:22, which says, "*The punishment of your iniquity, O daughter of Zion, is accomplished ...*" The word we translate as "*accomplished*" is the Hebrew word *tamam,* which can also mean "complete, finished, totally settled, made blameless."[2] The destruction that came upon God's people finished and settled the punishment for their past sin.

However, even this satisfaction of God's wrath was not a permanent solution — because guess what? The people weren't finished sinning. They would make more bad choices, and they would require more discipline. God had given them His law, including instructions for sacrificing animals to pay the penalty for sin, but Scripture tells us that even the law "*can never, by the same sacrifices that are continually offered every year, make [anyone] perfect*" (Hebrews 10:1). So the cycle would keep repeating: sin, judgment, repentance, restoration, sin, judgment ...

But everything changed when Jesus *"entered **once for all** into the holy places, not by means of the blood of goats and calves but by means of his own blood, thus securing an **eternal redemption***" (Hebrews 9:12, emphases added)!

• When He hung on the cross for our sins, Jesus said, *"It is finished"* (John 19:30). What did Jesus complete, finish, totally settle and make blameless in that moment when He gave up His spirit?

• How does Jesus' once-and-for-all sacrifice give you hope and joy today?

As we journey through Lamentations, let's build our own acrostic day by day. Write a sentence to the Lord, either your own lament or another kind of prayer based on today's scriptures, starting with the letter W.

DAY 24

Lamentations 5 takes on a slightly different pattern than what we've seen in the rest of the book. While there are still 22 verses (like the 22 characters of the Hebrew alphabet), this chapter is not an acrostic. It is shorter than the other chapters. Some scholars see this as an intentional and artistic way to show exhaustion. It is almost as though the author gave up trying to stay in the pattern he created from the beginning. However, this also may be a good form of "giving up" and surrendering to God; this chapter is the only chapter that is fully prayer.

Lamentations 5:1 says, "*Remember, O LORD, what has befallen us; look, and see our disgrace!*" Scholars agree that the word "*remember*" does not mean the poet wanted to inform the Lord of something He had forgotten (since God never forgets anything), but rather he wanted the Lord to see and act.

• In reading verses 1-14, what kinds of things do you see the poet asking God to "*remember*" and see (i.e., their homelessness, vulnerability, etc.)? Who had suffered?

BIBLICAL HIGHLIGHT:

Lamentations 5:7 says, "Our fathers sinned, and are no more; and we bear their iniquities." *This is not saying that innocent descendants were being punished for something they didn't do; rather, it points out that on top of any direct discipline from God, Jerusalem also experienced the consequences of their fathers' evil choices.*

As we hear the poet present this long list of sufferings to God, we may think, *Bad idea! Didn't the Israelites get into huge trouble with God for complaining about their circumstances in Bible stories like Numbers 14?* But let's look closer: This prayer is not complaining. The entire purpose of this prayer is to **believe in and call upon God's compassion**. Bible scholar Steven Smith points out that complaining is rooted in self-pity and is self-centered while lament prayers are rooted in brokenness and are God-centered.[1]

Second Corinthians 1:3 calls God the *"God of all comfort."* Psalm 103:13-14 says, *"As a father shows compassion to his children, so the LORD shows compassion to those who fear him. For he knows our frame; he remembers that we are dust."*

- Look up a definition for the word "compassion," and write it here.

The Lord is concerned about our suffering. He knows our weakness, our frailty. And in His time, He will act.

Through these verses in Lamentations 5, we see the complete breakdown of Israel's social structure. Families were torn apart (vv. 3, 7), elders and leaders were turned away or killed (v. 12), the most basic necessities for living came at a high cost (vv. 4, 9), women were not safe (v. 11), and men were worked to death (v. 13).

BIBLICAL HIGHLIGHT:

Lamentations 5:12 talks about how "no respect [was] shown to the elders" *in the fallen city of Jerusalem. Respect for elders was an absolute essential in Ancient Near Eastern culture.*[2] *Elders used their hard-earned wisdom to give advice and oversee affairs. Disrespect for elders, then, further demonstrated Jerusalem's desperate situation.*

This system of oppression was designed by Babylon to keep God's people weak and compliant.

- We, too, have an enemy who *"comes only to steal and kill and destroy"* (John 10:10). The devil will use whatever he can to make us weak and susceptible to his lies. But God has graciously given us ways we can stay strong against Satan's attacks. What are some ways that stand out to you in 1 Peter 5:8, James 4:7 and Ephesians 6:10-18?

The Lord sees everything. Every attack. Every hurt. Every pain. Every moment. He is there, and He cares.

- Today, take the time to bring your cares, concerns, difficulties and pain before the Lord. Lay them out — not to complain but to believe and call upon the compassion of God. What does God's compassion mean to you today? (If you need help with that last question, try looking up Hebrews 8:12, 1 John 3:1 or Zephaniah 3:9-20.)

As we journey through Lamentations, let's build our own acrostic day by day. Write a sentence to the Lord, either your own lament or another kind of prayer based on today's scriptures, starting with the letter X and/or Y.

DAY 25

As we come to the end of our study in Lamentations, let's talk about the role of faith when it comes to processing and expressing our emotions.

Lamentations 5:16 records an honest moment of confession: *"Woe to us, for we have sinned!"* Lamentations 5:17-18 records how the people recognized the effects of their sins: Their hearts had become sick, their eyes had grown dim, and the city of God's temple now lay desolate.

Then comes what Bible scholar Christopher Wright calls "an astounding leap of faith across the chasm of defeat, destruction, and death."[1] Verse 19 says, *"But you, O Lord, reign forever ..."*

•   In what ways is faith like leaping over a chasm? What are some chasms in your own life, and how might faith help you cross them?

Even in their faith, the people we read about in Lamentations still asked questions about suffering (v. 20). Faith doesn't give us all the answers. We can have faith that God is on the throne even if we do not understand why we are experiencing what we are. Even during Jerusalem's exile, which God's people understood was a consequence of their sin, the people didn't know when their suffering would end or what would happen next. And this is where Lamentations leaves us. It does not tie up the story with a nice, neat bow. There is no happy ending. The questions are not answered. In fact, the people of Jerusalem were wondering if their pain might just last *"forever"* (v. 20).

We can appreciate that this feels so similar to our human experience today. And it is OK, even in our faith, to acknowledge that in some moments, life hurts. It is OK to feel weak and tired.

- Like we see in Lamentations 5:22, sometimes our hope feels stretched thin, and we wonder if such a tiny speck of faith will hold us. Jesus once compared God's Kingdom to a tiny mustard seed. Yet what does Mark 4:31-32 say about that mustard seed?

Lamentations 5:21 says, *"Restore us to yourself, O LORD."* The word *"restore"* (in Hebrew, *sub*) means "to return or bring back."[2] In other words, the people's final cry was to be reunited with God.

This has been the cry of the human heart since the moment sin entered the picture. We are all separated from God by our sins, and none of us can reconcile ourselves back to Him. We remember this sobering fact when we read Lamentations 5:22: A holy, perfect God would be justified to *"remain exceedingly angry"* with us.

But instead ... He offers **free grace** and **eternal hope** in Christ.

The people in Lamentations could not see past their present pain, but we can pick up our Bibles and literally see all the pages that were yet to come. Pages that tell about a man named Jesus. Pages that talk of His life, death and resurrection, paying the price for our sins and bringing us back to the Father. These pages are proof that God answered — in bigger and better ways than we could ever imagine — the cry of Lamentations 5:21 to *"restore us to yourself, O LORD."*

- No matter what the current chapter of your life or the chapters leading up to this moment look like, how can you remind yourself that in Jesus, you have an eternity of pages coming in God's book?

Lamentations 5:15 says, "The joy of our hearts has ceased; our dancing has been turned to mourning." *Our pain is real. It's OK to express that. But our future with Jesus is equally real, and while our pain is temporary, our eternal hope is everlasting:* "[He] will turn [our] mourning into joy; [He] will comfort [us], and give [us] gladness for sorrow" *(Jeremiah 31:13).* **Come, Lord Jesus!**

Z

As we journey through Lamentations, let's build our own acrostic day by day. Write a sentence to the Lord, either your own lament or another kind of prayer based on today's scriptures, starting with the letter Z.

WEEKEND REFLECTION & PRAYER *Week 5*

Lamentations does not end with "... and they lived happily ever after." It says, "*Restore us to yourself, O LORD ... unless you have utterly rejected us, and you remain exceedingly angry with us*" (Lamentations 5:21-22). The end. Talk about raw emotions.

Maybe some of our emotions feel a little raw today too.

We have studied this week how sin tarnishes everything. It makes a mess. It causes pain. But praise the Lord that an eternal solution was offered to us in Christ Jesus! God answered His people's cry for restoration when He sent Jesus to live, die for sin, and conquer death through His resurrection. We are restored to our Father through faith in Jesus alone. And He will hold us and guide us through our emotions in a real and honest way as we turn our hearts and minds toward Him every day, every hour, every moment.

One last time, let's use a few verses from Lamentations to guide us in prayer together.

Lord God, our Maker and Redeemer, today we look at You ...

Lamentations 3:58 says, "O Lord; you have redeemed my life." *In You, Jesus,* "we have redemption through [Your] blood" *(Ephesians 1:7). You died so that we might live.*

[Call out to Jesus, your Redeemer. Hand Him your sin and pain. Accept the life He gives you.]

Lamentations 4:22 says, "The punishment of your iniquity, O daughter of Zion, is accomplished." *And as Jesus hung on the cross and gave His final breath, He said,* "It is finished" *(John 19:30). Thank You, Jesus, that Your sacrifice completely paid the price for our freedom.*

[Take a moment to praise the One who paid your debt, once and for all.]

Lamentations 5:19 says, "But you, O LORD, reign forever; your throne endures to all generations."

[Declare over all your circumstances, feelings, relationships and choices that **our God reigns.**]

My Lord, my Redeemer, I fix my eyes on You today. Thank You for showing us in Lamentations that we can come to You honestly. We can lay our broken and bruised hearts at Your feet. Help us to walk away from this study seeing Your love and grace and believing that Your response to our suffering was the sending of Your Son. Oh, what a Savior!

In Jesus' name, amen.

Notes

Notes

Notes

Notes

CAN I BE HONEST?

But this I call to mind,
& therefore I have hope:

The steadfast love of the Lord never ceases; his mercies never come to an end; they are new every morning; great is your faithfulness.

Lamentations 3:21-23

BIBLICALLY *Expressing* EMOTIONS

Emotions can be messy and confusing. Bob Kellemen, a former professor of biblical counseling at Faith Bible Seminary, talks about ways we can express our feelings in a way that honors God.[1,2] These same principles are evident throughout Lamentations as well.

First, there are two unbiblical ways to express emotion:
out-of-control expression and over-controlled suppression.

Out-of-control expression means indulging all our feelings without any filter. It is what the Apostle Paul warned against in Ephesians 4:19 when he said people had sinfully "*given themselves up to sensuality.*" They did whatever they felt. Feelings became their god instead of their feelings directing them toward God.

Over-controlled suppression means stuffing our feelings down or pretending they don't exist. Paul also called this out in Ephesians when he said, "*Be angry and do not sin*" (Ephesians 4:26). Though it is not OK to sin, it is OK to acknowledge anger. Denial or self-deception toward our feelings does not work.

> **Where we see this in Lamentations:** Lamentations is not a rant or an unmeasured outburst of feelings. It is a carefully constructed expression directed to God (e.g., "*O LORD, behold my affliction*" [Lamentations 1:9]). Yet the poet also did not suppress the very real hurt and pain he and others felt (e.g., "*For these things I weep; my eyes flow with tears ...*" [Lamentations 1:16]).

Second, God's Word teaches us to examine our feelings with spiritual eyes of wisdom, not worldly eyes of folly.

The psalmist in Psalm 73:16-17 says, *"But when I thought how to understand this, it seemed to me a wearisome task, until I went into the sanctuary of God; then I discerned their end."* When we bring our emotions to God, we can start to view them from an eternal perspective. When we look at our feelings through the eyes of this temporary world, we just mull them over and over, spinning in defeat.

Where we see this in Lamentations: In Lamentations 2:17, the poet acknowledged *"the LORD has done what he purposed; he has carried out his word which he commanded long ago."* Because God's people had sinned against Him, He faithfully carried out the consequences He had given them. In acknowledging this, the poet gained an eternal perspective on their suffering. Wisdom is found in having a correct eternal perspective.

Third, God's Word teaches us to confess emotions that are rooted in sin or lead to sin.

If we suppress our feelings, we can't confess the ones that may be tied to sinful attitudes in our hearts — but expressing our emotions in a biblical way can open the door to confession. We need to examine our feelings for *"bitterness and wrath and anger ... along with all malice"* (Ephesians 4:31). Then we can bring any sinful feelings to the Lord, also confessing our need for Him.

Where we see this in Lamentations: Lamentations 3:40-42 echoes this principle in saying, *"Let us test and examine our ways, and return to the LORD! Let us lift up our hearts and hands to God in heaven: 'We have transgressed and rebelled ...'"*

Fourth, we can make the choice to trust in God's sufficiency over self-sufficiency.

Facing our moods forces us to come face to face with our own insufficiency. Sometimes we feel we are at the mercy of our feelings. We dislike feeling powerless. But the truth is *we need God.* On our own, we truly are powerless to change our hearts, and we are powerless against the effects of sin — but the Holy Spirit fills us with His power (2 Timothy 1:7). God can help us navigate our emotions and feelings in a healthy, God-honoring way.

Where we see this in Lamentations: The poet who wrote Lamentations also understood that the only way through his feelings was with the help of the Lord. This is why he says in Lamentations 3:24, *"'The LORD is my portion,' says my soul, 'therefore I will hope in him.'"* God is our portion. He is our hope. We need Him, and we can rely on Him to help us through.

ENDNOTES

Life in Israel at the Time of Lamentations

[1] Parry, Robin. "Lamentations and the Poetic Politics of Prayer." *Tyndale Bulletin*, 62.1, 2011. pp. 65-88.

Lament Defined

[1] "Lament." Thompson, Jeremy. *Bible Sense Lexicon: Dataset Documentation.* (electronic ed.) Bellingham, WA: Faithlife, 2015.

[2] "Lament." Dictionary.com, https://www.dictionary.com/browse/lament.

Poetic Structure of Lamentations

[1] *The ESV Study Bible.* Wheaton, IL: Crossway, 2008. p. 1477.

Week 1

DAY 3

[1] Wright, Christopher. *The Message of Lamentations (The Bible Speaks Today Series).* Downers Grove, IL: InterVarsity Press, 2015. p. 64.

DAY 5

[1] Sproul, R.C. "Sin is Cosmic Treason." *Renew Your Mind,* Ligonier, March 1, 2021. www.ligonier.org/learn/articles/sin-cosmic-treason.

Week 2

DAY 7

[1] Lalleman, Hetty. *Jeremiah and Lamentations.* Tyndale Old Testament Commentaries. Downers Grove, IL: InterVarsity Press. p. 345.

Week 3

DAY 13

[1] Evans, Tony. "When God Lets You Hit Rock Bottom." Tony Evans: The Urban Alternative. https://go.tonyevans.org/blog/when-god-lets-you-hit-rock-bottom.

DAY 14

[1] Wright, Christopher. *The Message of Lamentations (The Bible Speaks Today Series).* Downers Grove, IL: InterVarsity Press, 2015.

[1] Kayser, Phillip G. "Lamentations." Biblical Blueprints, October 20, 2019. https://kaysercommentary.com/Sermons/BibleSurvey/22%20Lamentations.md.

DAY 15

[1] TerKeurst, Lysa. *Unglued: Making Wise Choices in the Midst of Raw Emotions.* Grand Rapids, MI: Zondervan, 2012.

DAY 16

[1] Parry, Robin. *Lamentations.* Two Horizons Old Testament Commentary, Grand Rapids, MI: Eerdmans, 2010. p. 106.

DAY 17

[1] "Sovereignty of God: Definition and Summary." *The Gospel Coalition.* https://www.thegospelcoalition.org/topics/sovereignty-of-god/.

DAY 19

[1] Leaf, Caroline [@drcarolineleaf]. Instagram, 9 Aug. 2022, https://www.instagram.com/p/ChCmb-NOfJr/.

DAY 22

[1] Smith, Steven. *Exalting Jesus in Jeremiah and Lamentations.* Christ-Centered Expositions, edited by David Platt, Daniel L. Akin and Tony Merida. Nashville, TN: B&H Publishing Group, 2019. p. 290.

[2] Huey, F.B. *Jeremiah, Lamentations.* The New American Commentary, vol. 16. Nashville, TN: Broadman & Holman Publishers, 1993. p. 481.

DAY 23

[1] Thompson, Jeremy. *Bible Sense Lexicon: Dataset Documentation.* (electronic ed.) Bellingham, WA: Faithlife, 2015.

[2] Swanson, J. *Dictionary of Biblical Languages with Semantic Domains: Hebrew (Old Testament)* (electronic ed.) Oak Harbor: Logos Research Systems, Inc., 1997.

DAY 24

[1] Smith, Steven. *Exalting Jesus in Jeremiah and Lamentations.* Christ-Centered Expositions, edited by David Platt, Daniel L. Akin and Tony Merida. Nashville, TN: B&H Publishing Group, 2019. p. 300.

[2] Lalleman, Hetty. *Jeremiah and Lamentations.* Tyndale Old Testament Commentaries, Downers Grove, IL: InterVarsity Press. p. 372.

DAY 25

[1] Wright, Christopher. *The Message of Lamentations (The Bible Speaks Today Series).* Downers Grove, IL: InterVarsity Press, 2015. p. 157.

[2] Swanson, J. *Dictionary of Biblical Languages with Semantic Domains: Hebrew (Old Testament)* (electronic ed.) Oak Harbor: Logos Research Systems, Inc., 1997.

Biblically Expressing Emotions

[1] Kellemen, Bob. "Emotions: Gone Bad and Mad." RPM Ministries, March 31, 2014. https://rpmministries.org/2014/03/emotions-gone-bad-and-mad-2/.

[2] Kellemen, Bob. "Emotions: Biblical and Unbiblical Ways to Handle Our Feelings." RPM Ministries, April 2, 2014. https://rpmministries.org/2014/04/emotions-biblical-and-unbiblical-ways-to-handle-our-feelings/.

Thank you for studying Lamentations with us, friend! We pray your time in God's Word has brought you hope and encouragement even as you process sometimes difficult emotions.

It's normal for all of us to feel fear, worry, anxiety and grief at times. And sometimes we have feelings that surprise us in their intensity. But some feelings we have might be more concerning, and we wonder whether we have the tools to process them on our own or whether we might need help.

In cases like that, it's good to talk to a doctor, professional counselor or therapist. A professional can help if your emotions feel all-consuming, cause you overwhelming or prolonged distress, or make it hard to fulfill your daily obligations.

If you would like a trusted recommendation for help, you can find professional resources at: https://proverbs31.org/about/counseling-support.

God bless you,
Your friends at Proverbs 31 Ministries

about
PROVERBS 31
MINISTRIES

> *She is clothed with strength and dignity;*
> *she can laugh at the days to come.*
>
> PROVERBS 31:25

Proverbs 31 Ministries is a nondenominational, nonprofit Christian ministry that seeks to lead women into a personal relationship with Christ. With Proverbs 31:10-31 as a guide, Proverbs 31 Ministries reaches women in the middle of their busy days through free devotions, podcast episodes, speaking events, conferences, resources, and training in the call to write, speak and lead others.

We are real women offering real-life solutions to those striving to maintain life's balance, in spite of today's hectic pace and cultural pull away from godly principles.

Wherever a woman may be on her spiritual journey, Proverbs 31 Ministries exists to be a trusted friend who understands the challenges she faces and walks by her side, encouraging her as she walks toward the heart of God.

Visit us online today at proverbs31.org!

PROVERBS 31
ministries

WE'VE GOT A NEW STUDY JUST FOR YOU ...

Am I Doing This Right?

*How To Live Out Your Faith Through
the Wisdom Found in James*

AVAILABLE APRIL 2024 AT
P31BOOKSTORE.COM.